George L. (George Lynde) Catlin

Tit Bits for Travelers; or, Random Pages from a Reporter's Scrap Book

George L. (George Lynde) Catlin

Tit Bits for Travelers; or, Random Pages from a Reporter's Scrap Book

ISBN/EAN: 9783337210465

Printed in Europe, USA, Canada, Australia, Japan

Cover: Foto ©Andreas Hilbeck / pixelio.de

More available books at **www.hansebooks.com**

Tit Bits

FOR

Travelers;

OR

Random Pages

FROM A REPORTER'S SCRAP BOOK.

BY

GEO. L. CATLIN.

NEW YORK:
1870.

TO

THE AMERICAN TRAVELER,

Always restless, impatient, hungry, thirsty, sleepy, and anxious for something or other new wherewith to while away the tedium of a long journey—this book is respectfully inscribed.

THE HALCYON'S RETURN.

I

At break of day on an April morning the night express might have been seen dashing along fully on time toward the town of G——, ten miles distant. On that day opened the spring meeting on the Goodstone Course, which annually summoned together the inhabitants of a circuit of a hundred miles or more. It was a clear bright morn, and as one by one the awakening passengers, throwing aside mufflers and robes and great coats and shawls, sat up, rubbed their eyes, and, brushing away the mist from the window panes, took in gradually the varied landscape, of dewy meadows, orchards, forests, farm houses and an occasional hamlet, and finally let their glance rest upon the bright grey dawn in the east, they thought, " 'Twill soon be day, and a fair day at that; we must be near to G——."

All phases of human character were represented in the half-waking, half-sleeping assemblage.

There was the old miller who had his fifty barrels of fine wheat flour on the freight car forward, and who, at an early hour that morning had given up his seat to a poor woman who had got on at a station where the train had stopped. He—good natured soul—had snoozed away the balance of the night on the top of some mail bags, and now, that morning broke, had returned to look up his overcoat and umbrella. But the poor woman was asleep and he wouldn't disturb her, he thought, until the train stopped. Then, on another seat away up forward were two young fellows all the way from H——, collegians home for the spring holidays, and ready for any amount of roguery. Early in the evening they had been casting sheep's eyes toward two or three pretty young ladies of G——, returning home from school under the charge of a very stupid old professor, who did nothing but nod and snore all the night long, leaving his fair *protegées* to return or repel the glances of the collegians as best they chose. But now, where these young ladies sat, it were difficult to determine, save by the presence of an auburn ringlet falling over the back of the seat, or by just the least little tip of a dainty foot visible on the floor below. They were sleeping soundly, these girlish, innocent creatures, little caring for the rollicking students, dreaming only of parents, brothers and sisters, who in an hour more would welcome them home again.

A louder snore than usual from the professor was followed by a rough, coarse remark from somewhere about the center of the car, where until after midnight, a party of four men, all wearing jewelry and moustaches, and quite elegantly dressed, had been playing cards, talking and laughing very loudly the while. But they, too, had finally sunk to sleep, and one of them, to tell the truth, had snored quite as loudly as the poor professor for awhile. But now they, too, were awake, and pulling out their watches expressed the opinion that the day would be a good one.

A baby here began to cry vociferously near the rear end of the car, much evidently, to the embarrassment of the young father, who, with high hat awfully battered during the hours of sleep, took it from the mother's arms, vainly endeavoring by a series of gyrations and jumpings to soothe the infantile grief. The yelling was contagious. Four or five other babies, summoned by the cries of the first one back to this world of milk and merriment, incontinently set up a screaming which effectually awoke every one, including the poor woman, who humbly thanked the kind miller for his overcoat, and handed him it with the green cotton umbrella he had left there.

The school girls awoke, too, looking pretty, though terribly in disorder, and laughed as they pinched the professor, telling him it would soon be time to alight. The collegians ceased their ogling after the green glasses of the awaking protector had gleamed once upon them. The young father once more resigned the screaming infant to its mother's care. The men with moustaches commenced to talk loud again, and lo—in that car but an half hour before full of insensible humanity, everybody was now awake save one. Rack-a-tack, rack-a-tack, clang-a-rang, clang-a-rang, incessantly went the wheels as the train dashed on to its destination; but it was not until the cars gradually slackened their speed, as they neared the platform, and the portly conductor, with extinguished lantern, came passing upon feet accustomed to steadiness, through the car, and cried out in stentorian tones, "Fifteen minutes for breakfast at G——," that a gray haired soldierly-looking man, who had been long awake, supporting upon his shoulder some one sleeping enveloped in his great cloak, lifted that cloak, and bending his head, whispered gently:

"Kate, my daughter, here we are."

The busy manufacturing town of G——, looking out upon an estuary of the sea, and overshadowed from behind by high, forest-clad hills, was remarkable for its beauty, its healthfulness, its prosperity. From daylight to dark on six days of the week, might be heard along its narrow, old-fashioned streets, the incessant clatter of machinery, the rattling of innumerable spindles, the screeching of whistles, the ringing of bells and all those busy sounds betokening a city of toil. Down at the wharves, great ships from the Indies, (for once upon a time its trade with the Bahamas and Antilles was not inconsiderable,) or from other foreign lands, lay moored, and all day long one might hear the "heave yo" of the stevedore laboring away in the hold, or of the sailors toiling away at the capstan chains or spreading snowy sails as their vessel, outward bound, turned prow down toward the sea. But on the seventh day quiet and still were the streets, save when, from a dozen spires and belfries, rang out the church bells, and when simultaneously from hundreds of neat, cosy homes issued the inmates on their way to the places of worship.

This, then, was G——, a prosperous, well regulated community, undisturbed the year round by hurtful excitements, connected daily with the rest of the world by three railroad trains, boasting three good hotels, a telegraph office and a morning newspaper; and this was the town where, on the morning our story opens, the express train, slackening its speed, came to a stop and discharged its now fully awakened passengers.

It was early, yet the platform was full of people. How enviably at home these people always appear to be whom the traveler finds awaiting the train in any strange town where he may arrive. Hackmen and express agents predominated, as usual, but beside these there were any number of people looking for expected friends. The pretty school girls found fathers and brothers to overwhelm them with kisses, while the professor stood stupidly by. A rough-looking mechanic, a little tipsy, gruffly thanked the portly miller for his kindness to the poor woman, his wife, and the father, with the dilapidated hat, hurried the baby and its mother off into an old fashioned country carriage that stood waiting for them behind the station. The students made a straight line for the nearest hotel, the moustached men for a neighboring ale house. And among the last of the passengers came the military-looking gentleman, his cloak buttoned up close to his throat, himself looking very stately and dignified as, supporting upon his arm a young girl, deeply veiled and in mourning, he handed her to a carriage, got in himself and said " To the Wilton House, driver."

On this eventful morning, the whole town had arisen early, and already the streets were alive with people. Tradesmen stood in their doorways rubbing their hands complacently, and promising themselves a brisk day. Horses and vehicles were never so numerous on the streets. Flags were flying in the public square and at different points along the principal thoroughfares. Here and there one met a jolly inebriate whose festivities had commenced early on the previous night. In short, for the nonce, all G—— seemed upside down with merry anticipation; for had not four of the finest stables in the State arrived, and was not the coming sport spoken of by old Granis' the turf oracle of the town, as the greatest ever known in that section? But it was at the hotels, in the offices where trunks and valises were piled up half way to the ceiling, and where the porters and waiters ran hither and thither in frantic haste, that the excitement which had possessed the town became most apparent The register at the Wilton House, a four-story brick building, facing directly upon the shaded square, showed already an arrival of three-score guests and over; when amid the din, might have been heard the voice of the clerk, calling out in stentorian tones to the headwaiter:

"Smith, are those rooms on the first floor ready for Major Loring?"

"All ready, sir," was the reply bawled out over the shoulders of half a dozen.

"Show him and his daughter up at once when they come," said the clerk.

Just then came the rattling of wheels, a carriage drove up, and the military-looking gentleman alighting took his daughter's arm again in his, paid the coachman, and the two, preceded by the waiter were ushered up stairs to the apartments engaged for them. There was a neat little parlor looking out upon the street, the window shaded with white lace curtains, the walls white and clean, the furniture complete, and the whole air of the room cosy and comfortable in the extreme. And off from the far end of it opened a door connecting with a darkened bed room, which in turn opened upon another, each of them newly made up from the chambermaid's hand, each telling of a tranquil repose.

All this, father and daughter surveyed before a word was uttered.

"Oh! how nice everything is, isn't it father?" exclaimed she. I am sure we are doing much better than I had anticipated."

The kind paternal face relaxed into a smile, as it looked down into hers.

"There, my darling," said the major, "that is the first good smile of happiness I have seen on your face for many a day. And go look in the mirror; upon my word, the morning air has made your cheeks as rosy as I remember they used to be when you were a child, and I took you walking over the hills with me every morning before I went off for so long."

"Ah, father, I remember it so well, and how good you were, lifting me over the muddy places, and risking your dear old eyes among the briers to pick me the prettiest hedge roses. Papa, you were not old then. No indeed you weren't; I can't realize that you are now. Do you know you have always looked the same to me, and always will—always my father, nothing less?"

"Yes, yes; I know it, Kate," said he, "but these white hairs make me have strange thoughts sometimes," and with another fond look, and a good-natured laugh, as if to offset the tear which her dear words had called forth, the major threw aside his heavy cloak, took off his hat and stood before the fireplace, a man tall, erect, florid of countenance though gray of locks, and scrupulously neat in dress withal, notwithstanding his journey.

"I have been thinking, Kate," said he, after a few moments, to his daughter, who was looking out upon the busy street abstractedly, "I have been thinking that you require rest. Now, lay aside your things, and let me leave you for a little while. You are tired, I know. I will ramble through the town for an hour or so, and be back in time to breakfast with you by 9 o'clock.

She turned and came toward him. "Don't stay long, dear father," she answered, standing before him and looking up, "I don't feel as if I could sleep a bit. But order the trunks sent up, and I will have everything to rights when you return."

"Oh! you little puss, I know you too well to suppose you will be idle. Don't you recollect that one of the first promises your childish lips ever lisped was that when you grew older, you would sew the buttons on my coats and keep my book-case in order for me? So now, bring me my cloak. I'll not be gone long, Kate."

She brought what he asked, and kissed her father good-bye, as resuming once more his stateliness of bearing, he passed out along the hall and descended the stairs to the street.

II.

"Why, Loring, is it possible," exclaimed a cheery voice, as the major, having called at the office to order the trunks sent up, sauntered leisurely up the street. He had been stationed in G—— many years before as recruiting officer when he was a young lieutenant; and the busy town, allowing for its growth and progress meanwhile, was not this morning altogether unfamiliar to him. He was recalling with some interest the events of his younger days passed here, when suddenly the friendly voice addressed him; and turning, he saw a middle aged individual, stout and short of stature, with rubicund, smooth shaven face, a merry twinkling eye, hair just turning the least bit grey, and hand extended to greet him. The major surveyed him from head to foot. He saw a dapper little man dressed in a black suit, scrupulously brushed, with silk hat, smooth and shiny, with boots brilliantly polished, with shirt bosom immaculate, and a standing collar so remorselessly starched that it had, even at that early hour, irritated the fat folds of the wearer's neck to a fiery redness. This good-natured, comfortable little man wore kids, one of which was upon his left hand, holding the other, as he extended his ungloved right in salute. "Why, old friend, don't you know me?" said he.

The major looked hard at him the while, and the play of his handsome features, as recognition gradually came with the glance, was worthy of a painter. "Why," said he, grasping the hand offered him, "as I live, this must be my old friend Tom Sparrow," and as the little corpulent man in black, overjoyed by the recognition, only shook the major's hand with redoubled vigor, the greeting became a most emphatic one, and the two looking into each other's faces, forgot in the pleasure of their re-union all the changes time had wrought thereon.

"I knew 'twas you," said the little man,—"was walking with my wife on the other side, two squares below when I spied you; wife was going to see about a birthday present for Jack, our oldest boy; Jack is eighteen to-morrow; just got home from college this morning. Well, I saw you; said I to wife, 'There's Bob Loring, by Jove,' and off I darted. She begged me to stop. 'Tom,' said Mrs. S., 'you are forever running off on wild goose chases after people, and making such ridiculous mistakes.' 'Nonsense wife,' said I, 'its Bob Loring, or I'll lose my next case,' so off I hurried after you, leaving estimable Mrs. Sparrow to wait my return. Come now, come with me. Loring, I'll introduce you."

The dignified major felt the little short fat arm locked with his, and himself hurried off at a rapid gait, laughing at his companion's good natured loquacity.

"And now tell me dear old friend, how has time dealt with you since we parted?" asked the latter, as he hastened with the captive major to join his spouse.

"The old story, Tom," replied Loring, "losses and gains, pleasures and pains. I have traveled some, seen a great deal of active service, and am now on the retired list. I've got a confounded Mexican bullet, fired at

Vera Cruz, in my left shoulder to this day, and can assure you I feel it on crisp mornings such as this."

"And your family? you married didn't you? Seems to me I heard of your wedding, through that captain of yours who relieved you here."

A shadow of gloom came over the major's countenance. "Yes," he answered, "my boy Will is off on the plains, a lieutenant in the —th. Kate, my daughter, is here with me. My wife was—"

"Now, Mr. S.," interrupted a voice, as good natured as that possessed by the one addressed, "I do protest against desertion."

"Not when I bring in such a prisoner, wife," replied the husband, letting go of the major's arm—"Mrs. Sparrow, let me, as the result of my wild goose chase, present my valued acquaintance, Lieutenant, (no, Colonel, by this time, I suppose,) Robert Loring," and all three bowed, the major gallantly lifting his hat, laughing, and interposing "Major Loring, Tom." He extended his hand to a matronly, rosy faced lady, a feminine counterpart of her lord, who stood benignly stroking his chin with his left hand, and daintily holding the lapel of his coat with his right.

"I am most happy, madame," said the major, "to meet the wife of my friend of long ago.

"And I feel that we are acquainted already, sir," she answered, "so familiar has your name become by my husband's frequent mention of the days when you were intimate. You are but a temporary visitor in G——, I presume. May we not claim you as our guest?"

"I am accompanied by my daughter, and have taken rooms at the Wilton House," said the major, "I must therefore decline an invitation, which, were I alone, would only be too gladly accepted as an opportunity for recalling the memories of a happy past."

"Bring her, too," interrupted the little man. "It will only make us the happier—I won't listen to a refusal."

"I must positively decline," said the major, in a manner which, while kind and courteous, left no doubt as to its finality.

"At all events, major, you will accompany us with your daughter, to the races, this evening, and take tea with us afterward, won't you?" asked she, good naturedly.

"With all my heart, madame," was the reply.

"We shall call for you at two, then," said Sparrow, pulling out from mere force of habit when any hour was mentioned, a huge gold repeater, which he was wont to say had belonged to his grandfather, who "fought the Hessians, sir, by Jupiter, and when thrown into their hands as a prisoner of war, had secreted it in his boot, sir, where it had remained, would you believe it, sir, until his recapture." All this he would have gone on to tell the major then and there, but that a touch on the elbow made him pause. "At two, sharp, remember," he said—"splendid sport in prospect. I've entered a colt myself for the two mile dash. Good bye till then major," and as the matron bowed in departing, the happy little man bowed too and went sailing off complacently by her side, while the major, erect and dignified as ever, looked after them pleasantly as they went, and then noting the hour, turned his steps toward the hotel, where Kate, having fulfilled all her promises, by unpacking and setting matters to rights, was seated by the window awaiting her father's return. And when his measured step was heard along the corridor, a door flew open, a fair young face, shaded with golden ringlets, peeped out, a pair of soft blue eyes looked affectionately into his, and two rosy lips, upturned for welcome, exclaimed: "Oh, papa, I'm so glad you have come. Now, off with your hat and cloak. There," and suiting the action to the word, she unhooked the high collar, and threw off the cloak, reached up and lifted the hat from his head, hung them up in the bed-room, and pointing to a newspaper lying upon the chair where she had been sitting, said: "See here, papa."

"What is it, daughter, that you have as a surprise for me? Nothing bad about your brother, I hope—no more Indian fights, eh?" said the major hurriedly.

"No. But see; read for yourself, father;" and she brought him the paper, putting her finger upon a paragraph. "What to think of it I hardly know."

Young as she was, he had since her childhood, acceded to her every wish and opinion that respect which he felt alone could win her implicit confidence in return; nor had his judgment been at fault. She made it her religion to believe as he believed, to think as her father thought, to do as he did, and he in return had found growing with her years a discernment and common sense which had now come to be indispensable to him in his conclusions on any important subject. Father and daughter, mutual confidents, mutual advisers, neither of them felt that the counsels of the other could be spared, and so it was that when she eagerly brought him the newspaper and pointed out a paragraph in the ship-news column, telling him she was at a loss to know what to make of it, he well knew there was moment in the subject.

There came just then a rap on the door: "Will Major and Miss Loring take breakfast in their own, or in the breakfast room?"

"Here," said Kate; "for, papa, I want to have a good talk with you on this subject and know what you think of it. Please serve breakfast here," she continued, addressing the waiter.

The door was gently closed and the major read:

"By advices from New York received by merchants in this place, we learn that the Europa arrived there yesterday from Liverpool after a stormy passage of fourteen days and ten hours. Her officers report that on the 18th inst., while nearing the Banks they spoke the brig Halcyon, bound hither from Calcutta, but driven far out of her course by the heavy southerly gales which had prevailed for ten days previous. All hands on board were well, and expressed themselves confident of being able to reach this port in safety. Among her passengers, also, her consignees here are informed, are three survivors of a vessel (name not known) lost eighteen months since in the Indian Ocean. The Halcyon's arrival may be daily looked for."

All the while he had been reading, Kate, with anxious eyes, had been looking up into his face. When he came to the end, each for a moment looked doubtingly, inquiringly, at the other.

"Shall we—can we dare hope, father?" she said. He thoughtfully, hesitatingly answered, smoothing the silken hair back from her forehead, "Why hope to be disappointed, my child? I fear 'twould be hoping against hope. Could I but credit for one moment that your dear mother, surviving the horrors of that fearful night, were still alive—but no—ah! why think of it? And yet, Kate, 'tis possible—"

"Can we suffer more keenly than we have suffered, papa?" she said. "Are not these lingering doubts more tormenting than the undisguised certainty? Let us in our hearts pray for courage to meet this new agony of expectancy, and to bear the new disappointment that may await us."

"But did not the mate see the boat in which we had placed her, go down not a hundred yards from the ship?"

"And the mate cannot be relied upon, father. You remember how intoxicated he and many others of the crew were?"

Rap, rap, rap was heard on the door, and the waiter entered with the preliminaries for breakfast.

"I will find the Halcyon's agents after breakfast," said the major. "Meanwhile, my darling, be patient, be hopeful, and let not your, returning life and animation be clouded over by these gloomy remembrances. I have met this morning an old acquaintance, Tom Sparrow, a lawyer here. He and his wife invited us to become their guests. This I declined, for I know your wishes in such cases. But they will call at two o'clock and take us with them to the Goodstone races.

"Do you really wish me to go, papa?" said Kate, sitting down to the table.

"Yes, I should like it," he said; "I believe it will do you good."

"At two, you say, papa?"

"At two, my daughter," and then the major too sat down to his coffee, and talked off-handedly, while in reality only thinking of the Halcyon.

III.

"Marables & Weir," said a musty sign, displayed over the doorway of a shipping office on the street which ran along the water side of G——. Water Street it would have been called of course anywhere else, but in this particular town it went by the name of Lighthouse Street, for the reason that from old times, when G—— was an aspiring village, this road, now a busy street, had been flanked at either end by a light which many a mariner, far out from shore, had blessed on stormy winter nights.

Everybody knew where Marables & Weir's place was on Lighthouse Street. Everybody knew they had ships sailing to or coming from a dozen ports, in as many different countries. "Old Man Marables," as every one called him, had once been a merchant captain himself, but, years before, tired of the sea, had turned over the command of his ship, the Good Hope, to his son, and taken himself to a little office upon the site of the present one, where with advancing time came new gains and new ships, until he had taken in his son-in-law, Harry Weir, as a partner who in reality managed the business, and put up that now musty sign, "Marables & Weir." Their office was a dingy, old-fashioned place, partitioned off with glass from the rest of the establishment, where oakum, cables, chains, pulleys and anchors were strewn about, and where a strong odor of tar was invariably prevalent. Of all these outer domains, a one-legged porter, who had sailed half a dozen voyages with the captain, before losing his leg in slipping the anchor one day, had charge. Within the ancient and sacred precincts of the office itself, with its old-fashioned furniture and clock were the partners and the book-keeper, guarded from needless intrusion by a placard upon the door, informing outsiders that only business would be tolerated as a reason for admittance.

On this particular morning the office appeared to be the scene of no unusual activity. The captain had his glasses on and was seated by the door, carefully reading the newspaper. The book-keeper, an old sallow looking fellow, with long hair, and a countenance which seemed to say "Oh, how I'd enjoy a fortnight in the country," sat by the window, biting the end of his pen-handle and vacantly gazing out upon the water. Harry Weir had just gone out on business; he was active and talkative enough, and, it may in fact, be said was the life and soul of the establishment, for the captain had come to be crusty and fearfully profane withal, in his old age, and the poor book-keeper, with a large family to eat his salary up in bread and butter, had no time to laugh and be merry.

"There's the Widgeon," said he, suddenly breaking the silence, "just coming to anchor in the stream."

"What?" said Marables gruffly. He had a kind heart, but, like a good many with kind hearts, a strange way of showing the fact.

"You were asking about the Widgeon, a while ago," replied the book-keeper mildly. "She is here, and I see Nalley coming ashore in the boat,"

The old man without replying folded his paper and went to the window. "Ah!" said he, having satisfied himself; "now perhaps we shall hear something. Go on the wharf, Simmons, and ask him to step over here when he lands."

The dyspeptic book-keeper seized his hat, and, darting for the door to obey the direction, almost ran into somebody just entering. It was the major.

"Is Mr. Marables in the office?" he inquired.

"That is Capt. Marables, sir," said the book-keeper resuming his errand.

Major Loring bowed, "I have come for information in regard to the brig Halcyon, which I learn is consigned to you," he said.

The captain pointed to a sailor-looking man, with rough beard and short legs, who was just crossing the street toward the office, "Here comes a pilot, just up from below, who can tell us all about it," said he.

The major turned his eyes in the direction named, and saw the two as they entered the office. "Well, Cap'n," said the newly arrived, seating himself.

"Nalley, what about the Halcyon? Any signs of her yet?" asked Marables.

"There was a brig in the offing last night at sundown but she can't get in until the wind changes. I think it's your brig."

"Umph!" said Marables looking at the major, who,

with hands folded behind him, was listening to the conversation. "And what do you think about the wind changing, Nalley?"

"Well, it's my opinion we shall have it from the south before the tide turns to-night. In that case the brig will be in by to-morrow noon. I'm going down again early in the morning to meet—Why, bless my stars, Capt. Loring, is that you, sir?" and the sturdy salt doffed his hat which up to that time had shaded his eyebrows and face, and rising, saluted the major most respectfully. " Why, Capt. Marables," he continued, turning to the old merchant, who was rubbing his glasses preparatory to a more extended survey of his visitor. " Why, when I was in the marines, Capt. Loring was my commander, and a more gallant officer, though I say it to his face, never wore uniform."

"I am glad to meet you again, Nalley," said the major, extending his hand, "and how long have you been out of the service?"

"Four years or so, captain. You see, 'twas too lazy a life for me; half-sailor, half-soldier, yet not a bit of either, as 'twere. Nothing to do but eat and sleep; laughed at by the jacks when at sea, and envied by the infantry when ashore, I got heartily tired of the marine corps, and after serving two enlistments, left with five hundred dollars saved up, in my pocket. I am now the master of that pilot boat yonder. The Widgeon, I call her. But, captain, you've grown old-like since I saw you last. I remember well when you left us at the Brooklyn Navy Yard; when you were ordered off on foreign service, I mean; how the boys cheered you, and that little speech you made us all. There wasn't a dry eye in the company that time. It does my heart good to see you again."

"Those were happy days that you recall, Nalley," said the major, "but I fear that I am trespassing upon the time and good nature of these gentlemen. I will therefore briefly state the object of my visit. I arrived here this morning, Capt. Marables, with my daughter, for the purpose of attending the races. She has been in poor spirits of late, and I thought that the change would do her good. By to-day's paper, however, I learn that your brig, the Halcyon, brings as passengers, three survivors of a vessel lost in the Indian Ocean about a year and a half ago. Is it not so?"

"So we have been informed by a dispatch from our agents in Calcutta," said Capt. Marables.

"Sir," continued the major, "my daughter and I are survivors of such a ship-wreck. The steam packet Bombay, which ran on a rock and was lost in the same waters on the 23d of November, 186—, had on board as passengers, my wife, my daughter and myself, returning by the Company Route to the Mediterranean, where I was to join the Albermarle at Genoa. But two of us reached there;"

and the major's voice trembled, "my wife I last saw lowered over the sinking vessel's side into a boat, which, in another moment, was swept away into the darkness, and, it is said, capsized."

Respect for his grief kept the listeners silent, as the gray-haired major, still with tremulous voice though standing erect and proud before them, continued:

"We had long since given up hope, for although the sloop of war St. James shortly after cruised among the islands and over a circuit of a hundred miles thereabouts in search of survivors, it was all in vain. Hope was dead, gentlemen, until I read what I have this morning, and now you know it all. Now you must perceive the distressing uncertainty which tortures me."

"The cable dispatch," said Marables, "which brought us the intelligence concerning the Halcyon came by way of Liverpool, and was singularly inexplicit, giving no names or dates, barely the mention of the fact. When do you go down again, Nalley?"

The honest pilot jumped to his feet. "This hour, if Captain Loring wishes," said he.

"But it all depends upon the wind, remember, my man," said Marables, "where's the use of your beating about outside or laying at anchor on the bar all night, so long as the Halcyon is away off on the horizon. She can't get up to-night, can she?"

"Impossible," said Nalley, "but my boat is at Captain Loring's command."

The major thought a moment. "I thank you," said he, "and accept your kind offer. At six in the morning be ready to hoist your anchor. Meanwhile, should any necessity for an earlier departure transpire, send a message for me to the Wilton House." And with a courteous good morning, and a cordial grasp of the pilot's hand, the stately old major withdrew, and wended his way back to one of whose companionship he could not, since her mother's loss, long remain deprived.

There were visitors in the parlor, he observed as he trod the carpeted hallway. He heard the gentle voice of Kate, interrupted at intervals by the cheery chirrupings of Tom Sparrow. "No race to-day, Loring," said he, a gloom momentarily passing over his countenance, "no race to-day, my friend—postponed until the day after tomorrow—muddy tracks—too much for the horses, you know—severe disappointment—everybody talking about it—can't be helped, you know. Go to theatre to-night, though. Couldock and daughter play in 'Dora'—splendid thing, I'm told."

Thus the dapper little lawyer rattled on, while Kate anxiously looked at her father, to glean, if possible, an inkling of what he might have learned during his absence. But not a word did those features divulge, as the major, replying, said: "The postponement which you so much regret I do not, Tom, for to have fulfilled our engagement with you to-day would have been impossible.

By day after to-morrow, Kate (whose acquaintance I am glad to see you have made) and I may be in better mood to enjoy the sport."

Her blue eyes brightened when he said this. "Ah, father," she involuntarily exclaimed, "good news, I know it—good news."

"Be patient, my darling; to-morrow we shall know all."

"To-morrow? must we then wait until to-morrow, papa?" and to their visitor, who was bowing to depart, "you will dine with us, Mr. Sparrow, will you not?"

"Just as well as not," said he, "Mrs. S. has things upside down at home for John's birth-day party. She's booked you, major, for the first quadrille with her, so look up your dancing pumps, old fellow."

The major smiled. "Come," he said, "let us talk of old times, and all that has befallen us during the long years."

"With all my heart, Loring," and these two old friends, reunited after their long separation, sat down, face to face, recounting the joys, the sorrows, which departed years had brought, while Kate, sitting at her father's feet, forgot, in the varied recital, the cares and anxieties of the moment. But while they talked, there came a timid, quiet rap on the door. It opened, and the sallow face of Simmons, the book-keeper, peered in, looking around. "Is Major Loring in? Ah, yes; Major, Nalley says the wind is getting around, and it will be time to start in half an hour."

"Tell him I shall be punctual," said the major, looking at his watch.

IV.

Extracts from the diary of Mrs. Catharine Livingston Loring:

DECEMBER 27, 186—.

And where are they—that dear protector, that affectionate child? Through that terrible danger, that long illness, those dark moments, when death hovered over me, but this one thought has been mine: Are they still living, or have the merciless waves long since swallowed them up? Father in Heaven, have mercy—the wife, the mother, cries out to thee from the depths of her doubt and despair. Give her strength, give her patience, give her an unfailing, unfaltering trust in Thee. Give her to say, in grief or in joy, "Not my will, but Thine, O God! be done."

And once more I feel returning life. May it not be that life is given me for a more zealous guarding of my duty?

May it not be that the slender thread, awhile since so nearly riven in twain, may yet increase to a ligament binding me with tenfold strength to a life blessed by those dear ones restored to me?

Yet, I dread the answer so fraught with unspeakable sorrow or gratitude.

Patience, my heart; nerve thyself to whatever the future may bring. Trust and hope on, nor yet grieve for those who may even now themselves be mourning thee as forever lost.

They say we have been here nearly four weeks. 'Tis all a blank time to me. I recollect the parting kisses, as I was lowered into the boat, expecting them to follow me. Then I was suddenly in darkness;

the boat, lifted upon a great wave, was dashed from its fastenings, and in another moment the ship's lights were fast receding from our sight. Our cries were vain; the roaring of wind and wave, the screams of drunken and desperate men, the shrieks of women and the plaintive cry of that poor little infant, mingled with our beseechings. We were adrift, the second mate and we three women, sparsely clad, and wet and benumbed.

Let me think! Ah, no—I cannot recall the days and nights that followed. Thirst and hunger, and efforts almost superhuman, stand out as the only landmarks in that dreary waste of memory. Ah, yes! one event I distinctly picture. That poor English girl who died, talking of her mother! I shudder to think how pallid and distorted her face was when we two survivors, speechless, saw the mate consign her remains to the sea, then so tranquil and placid. I do remember, too, when the cry of "Land! thank God, land!" joyfully broke from the mate's lips; then—it seemed a long time after—the boat's bottom grated upon the sand. This is all that my memory brings back to me.

And to-day Sherburne, who has watched night and day by my side, as I lay on yonder pallet of grass, has told me all; has allowed me to sit up once more, providing for me this stool of twisted boughs, which he manufactured during my moments of sleep; has pointed out to me the spot where he hollowed a grave for her who survived with us the perils by water. This old book, drenched as it was, he found among the clothing dear Robert had thrown into the boat, and I now write with the same pencil which his dear hands placed there on the day we left port. How long ago that seems! And yet, 'tis not over five weeks ago.

I see a little white flag waiving from a staff upon the hill-top yonder, and Sherburne is standing there too. Poor fellow! How attentive, how respectful he has been. When my husband interposed on the Calcutta wharves that day to protect him from the American sailors, who had been drinking and were quarrelsome, how little did he anticipate this return. I cannot draw him into any extended conversation, save by constant questioning. "Yes, my lady," and "No, my lady," are his invariable answers. He brought me this morning two little fish he had caught by a peculiar line and hook of his own make. And here he has spread his jacket on the sand under my feet, lest I should be in danger from the dampness.

But can we find subsistence here on this island? Sherburne tells me he has explored it for a mile or so from the shore, and finds no traces of any human inhabitants. There is game in abundance, but we have no gun of any kind. He has, by the aid of his jack-knife, manufactured a long-bow, and twisted together linen threads into a bow string, and then, by arrows cut in the forest and sharpened at the fire, has succeeded, he says, in killing two good sized birds during my illness. A clear spring bubbles forth not a hundred yards away from me, and sends its pure waters trickling down the hillside to the seashore. By the aid of stakes and the timbers from our boat, he has built for me a tolerable shelter, thatching it with grass on the roof and sides. Poor fellow, he seems entirely forgetful of self in his desire to protect the wife of his chance benefactor.

Two months later the rainy season will set in, but ere that Sherburne will, he hopes, have completed our new abode on the hill-top. He is working hard, he tells me, in his leisure moments, and I have promised, so soon as my strength will permit, to give him all the assistance in my power.

But I see him coming down toward me again. Perhaps he has seen a ship. Three vessels have passed in sight, he says, since we landed. One of them, apparently a war vessel, came quite near in and fired a gun. Alas, we had no fire then, and our flag staff was not ready. We could make no signal in reply.

* * * * * * * *

JANUARY 18th, 186—.

Again I venture out from the damp, noisome darkness of yonder hut, and breathe the free, pure air, blowing fresh from the sea, which dances and sparkles before me. God is indeed good to me, in thus again sparing my life from the insidious fever which returned with increased vigor since I last wrote in these pages, only to leave me weak, irritable, and despondent.

Time wears on and brings us no succor. A small trading boat came in quite close to us last week, evidently intending to land, probably for water, Sherburne says, but the wind came up fresh from the eastward, and they went off to sea again. I am half disheartened, and can see in my companion's unhappy face what his lips will not confess. He has become an expert in the use of the bow and the line, and we do not want for provisions, which he takes good care to season with salt gathered on the rocks. I do not complain. I am but too thankful for these blessings. Yet, in my soul there is daily growing up a despair which at times all but drives me mad. I will not think of it.

The new house progresses but slowly. My illness, and the repeated calls upon his assistance, give Sherburne but little time to work uninterruptedly. He begins, too, now and then, to venture a wish that I would hurry and be well in order that I may help him. He needs me, he says, to carry the wood which he cuts, and to help him put it in position. But I am losing heart, and sometimes think that before the house is completed only one will remain to occupy it.

* * * * * * * *

JULY 30th.

My husband's birthday, and Sunday too. Sherburne, who is a precise old mariner, has kept a log since our arrival, religiously notching each day when he awakes in the morning.

The sun is very hot to-day, and I have sought shelter under a tree whose boughs, covered with luxuriant verdure and bending over to the ground, form a natural summer house. I know not why, but I am lighter of heart than for a long time past. Perhaps the spirits of those loved ones, still, I trust, in the land of the living, are recalling with mine the happy anniversary a year since, and are inspiring the while a mutual hopefulness. Perhaps, too, my restored health comes to give me new courage. 'Tis a wonder I survived that little hut with its pallet of grass.

Sherburne and I quarreled last week. For two days he was moody and morose, and on the third told me, abruptly, that he did not see how we were to get along hereafter; the birds were getting scarce, and very timid at that, and the fish would not bite. I saw he was cross. So was I; and I told him I did not believe what he said. How ungrateful it was of me. But I have come to be utterly selfish and pitiless here, I sometimes think. He answered me roughly and went off. I did not see him all that day; but next morning, before the cabin, lay a bird and two fishes. The next day, another bird and fish. The day after, he came to me, about noon, his eyes cast down, and begged forgiveness, saying he was not himself of late. The noble fellow! I shed tears myself and told him I owed my life to him. Since then he has been working harder than ever since our house was completed.

* * * * * * * *

August 21st.

Sherburne was taken ill with a violent fever this morning. He was away until very late in the night tending a signal fire, for we had seen a ship's masts on the horizon at sunset. Now he is lying restless on the floor here, breathing heavily and calling for water. This is the severest trial of all. There, I must put down my book, he is calling me.

* * * * * * * *

August 23rd.

I fear that my companion will not recover. Yesterday, after an absence of an hour or two, during which I fished with tolerable success, I found him raving in a delirium, which was followed at night by a stupor and weakness, in which he remained until morning. Before dawn, I heard him faintly calling me and begging for a drop of water. Then he told me, in a weak, faltering voice that he feared he would die. I bade him cheer up and hope, although my heart doubted the while. He fell asleep after I gave him to drink. This sleep may be the crisis. There—he is stirring.

* * * * * * * *

SEPTEMBER 1st.

Two weeks' watchings and labors have worn me out, and even as I write, it is with a hand so unsteady as to make my words scarcely legible. God be thanked; Sherburne is recovering, and to-morrow will, I think, be able to sit up once more. He is very grateful, and talks of nothing save his gratitude, utterly unmindful of his own past kindness to me.

* * * * * * * *

DECEMBER 2nd.

The anniversary of our landing—can it be that only a year has passed since then? A year—twelve succeeding months—made up of weary, monotonous days of expectancy. A year!—as I think of it, hope dies in me.

Yet I live; is not this a subject for thankfulness? Shall my grave be here on this desolate spot, or in the home of my early days, perchance beside those whose memory is ever uppermost?

Since the terrible equinoctial gale which leveled our abode, and had nearly ended our lives, hard work has driven off these thoughts which to-day return to me with a thousand fold more potency. Insensibly, of late, I find there has stolen over me a stolid indifference to all save the present; but at times, as now, the mist rises, and I see again the visions which hope was wont to picture. We see vessels passing more frequently now, for the trading season has set in, yet they either do not see us, or disregard our signals.

* * * * * * * *

CHRISTMAS DAY.

Was there ever a merrier one? Sherburne has just come breathlessly in from the signal post to tell me, in hurried words, that a large merchant vessel came in sight early this morning, and, bearing steadily in towards the island, has come to anchor about five miles away, the people on board evidently detecting his signals. A boat has put off toward shore. I cannot write more now, so eager am I to join him at the signal station.

   * * * * * * * *

I scarce know how to record my happiness, save upon my bended knees before that Heavenly Father who has preserved us through all these perils and privations. The boat's crew is from the English ship Hercules, bound for Bombay. They are kind and generous, and Sherburne is already a lion among them. But joy of joys! my first question was for information of the lost vessel — were the passengers saved? At first they did not remember, but one of the sailors finally told me that he had been in Bombay when the survivors, all of whom had been rescued by another vessel, had reached there, and then one or two of the others remembered the same circumstance. And can I dare hope that, after all this sad past, I shall yet again behold those dear faces and embrace that well-beloved husband and child? Father, forgive my moments of mistrust and despondency. Let that life, prolonged and made happy by Thy mercy, be dedicated anew to Thee.

V.

The Halcyon's voyage had been long and tedious. Now becalmed in glassy seas, now driven by adverse winds far out of her course; in doubling the Cape encountering a succession of furious gales, and thereby obliged to put in at Cape Town for provisions and repairs, it was not wonderful that, when at last she neared the Atlantic's western shores, all on board looked forward with eagerness to that moment when "Land, ho!" should be shouted from the masthead.

Among those whom she bore homeward to loving and loved ones were the two who, for a year, on that lonely isle, had, by the grace of God, lived through expectancy and hope to their deliverance. And as each day brought with it a nearer approach to the reunion which had been the dream of their absence, there came to each a vague dread lest, perchance, some fatal surprise might yet await them on arriving.

Yet, whatever might be in store, they were eager to know it all—good or bad, the sooner 'twere over the better. Impatience would not longer brook delay by wind and wave. One morning, while on the Banks of Newfoundland, a Cunarder, bound for New York, came rapidly up from astern, throwing the spray from her paddles and pushing gallantly on through the sea toward her destination; she passed close alongside, stopped her engine, and spoke the sailing vessel, whose passengers and crew, weary and impatient, heard the ding of the gong in the engine room as the ponderous machinery began to revolve again and the huge craft moved on once more, leaving a white foamy wake behind her. And as, a few hours later, she disappeared on the horizon, her course only marked by a column of black smoke rising against the sky, longing eyes became dimmed with tears, and one eager heart regretted that its possessor had not availed herself of that opportunity for a speedier solution of the doubts which tormented her.

So when, on the following day, another cloud of smoke was sighted astern, and in time the mast and funnels and hull of another steamer came successively in view, a signal was run up to the Halcyon's masthead, and the steamer, a Havre and New York liner, lay to in response, while a boat put off from the brig. Sturdy arms were at the oars, and in the stern, beside the steersman, sat the wife, the mother, braving all, daring everything, in the hope of sooner rejoining those who alone on earth were dear.

"Kate," said the major, as soon as the sallow-faced book-keeper who had come to deliver the pilot's summons had withdrawn, "I want you to take a sail down the harbor this afternoon. And you, too, Tom, will accompany us I hope. The skies are bright, the wind fair, and there is every prospect of a charming pleasure-trip. Nalley, the pilot, one of my old marines, whom I met this morning, has offered us his boat, the Widgeon, and I cannot refuse such an opportunity."

"A neater or faster craft of her tonnage doesn't sail in these waters," said Sparrow, who prided himself upon knowing everybody and everything in G——. "But I must decline, Loring, much as I should enjoy it. Mrs. S.

would never forgive me if I left her in the lurch at this emergency in her party-giving career. I see how it is the boat is waiting."

"*And*" said the major, "*the Halcyon is coming in with three survivors of the shipwreck which separated me from my wife, and this dear child from her mother.*"

Both started; Kate, her face flushed with eagerness, exclaimed, "Oh, papa, is it indeed so?" and hastened to make arrangements for departure. Nor did the fat little lawyer conceal his surprise at the announcement. "I read about it this morning," said he—" but little dreamed it interested you so deeply. Come, no ceremony, Loring, I'll come and dine with you to-morrow. God grant that your hopes may be realized. I know too, when I'm in the way, though you're too polite to say it. Good bye," and the father and daughter were alone.

"Take your fur cape and shawls, Kate," said the major, "we may need them, for it blows fresh and cool on the water. Are you nearly ready, daughter?"

"All ready, dear father," said Kate, bringing forth his hat and cloak. In the pocket of the latter she had quietly slipped the major's cigar case, full of his favorite Havanas, and into a little satchel she carried on her arm, an opera glass. "Now we can go. But"—and her countenance looked up, inquiringly, into his—"oh, father, I almost dread the denouement."

He, brave old man, had nerved himself to the errand.

His glance met her's tenderly, but there was not in it even a semblance of misgiving. "Cheer up, dear, dear child," said he, "we shall soon know now."

Nalley was awaiting them at the pier, abreast of which lay the Widgeon ready for the start, her white sails flapping in the afternoon wind. He bowed respectfully to Kate, as on her father's arm, she approached where he had been sitting. "Major, you're prompt, I see," said he. " The wind has deceived me for once. The Halcyon is not more than five miles off shore. On her next leeward tack we shall catch a sight of her. If you say so we will get aboard, and up anchor. I see the Fanny coming in to answer the signal for a ilot. If we don't take care, she will get the start of us."

The boat was awaiting them alongside the pier. A few strokes of the oars, and they shot rapidly over the calm water to the neat craft which was to bear father and daughter to joy or despair. "Up anchor" shouted Nalley, "never mind the boat, let her swing astern; haul taut on that jib sheet, boys; now the mainsail—so."

The orders were obeyed with an alacrity which convinced the major that his service in the marines had taught Nalley the blessing of discipline on shipboard. In another moment the light craft yielded to the influence of the gentle wind filling her canvass, and, careening lightly, moved away from her anchorage towards the mouth of the harbor, passing great ships, moored or at anchor, crumbling water-soaked wharves on which long time ago had been landed the wealth of foreign lands, then lawns and homesteads, then the lighthouse, then meadows water-lined with drift-wood, and casks and endless debris, then, on either side, sandy points extending out like two withered arms to embrace the open sea beyond, and forming a natural gateway to the beautiful harbor of G——.

All this time the major and Kate had been seated aft, glancing now and then at the varied view presented on either shore, yet more frequently shading their eyes to look toward the sea at that point where the brig should first come in view from behind the wooded highland which concealed her. Not a word spoke Nalley the while, as he stood with his hands holding the tiller behind him, and looking stolidly out ahead, apparently unconscious of the presence of his passengers. There were delicate sensibilities under that rough exterior which told him that silence would be more welcome than words. But when the boat went scudding out past the points, so close to the sandy beach that Nalley might have shied his hat high and dry ashore, and the fresh strong breeze which precedes the sunset filled the sails and sent the Widgeon dashing ahead like a race horse, Nalley, the seaman, had to speak. "Now we feel it, major," said he exultingly, "and yonder is the Halcyon; the Fanny has sent off a pilot, I see, but we shall be there now in ten minutes if this glorious breeze lasts."

"How exhilarating it is, papa, this cool, crisp salt wind, and how fast we are moving. Do you hear the water plashing under the bows. Oh, dear me, papa! its of no use. I can't conceal it. I never was so anxious—so much in suspense in my whole life. I scarcely dare look toward the vessel yonder. I am trembling with eagerness. How much longer will it be papa?"

Major Loring had risen, and was standing bareheaded, with his arms folded, looking mutely out over the intervening waters toward the Halcyon, upon whose decks forms of men were already visible. The wind was playing with his gray locks throwing them back in confusion, and in his eye there was the light of expectancy. Kate's question broke in upon his reverie.

"What did you ask, my darling?" he said, even more tenderly than was his wont, for in a few moments more she might be even dearer and more precious to him than ever.

"How much longer, papa?" she repeated timidly, looking up.

"Not long. Not long, my daughter. Look!" And as he pointed they saw the flutter of a woman's dress upon the quarter-deck of the brig.

"Here, papa," said Kate, hastily producing the glass from her satchel. "Use this, I brought it with me."

"Too far, yet," said he, adjusting and lifting it to his eyes.

"The Fanny's pilot has boarded her," said Nalley. "See! Down comes the blue bunting with the horse on it. I'll run up around her stern, and scud alongside in speaking distance." And, lifting his voice, "All hands forward, ready to 'bout ship."

The men came quickly up from the forward hatchway and stood in readiness. Already the dingy hull of the brig loomed up not two hundred yards away, as, with all sails set, she came plunging onward toward the termination of her long, long voyage. Men were standing at the bow, on the bowsprit and cross-trees, or were peeping out from the ports, eagerly straining their eyes toward the distant steeples and roofs and hillsides, gilded in the sunset.

And now the shadow of the brig shot over the pilot boat, while the roaring of the waters under her bow, and the flapping of the Widgeon's sails, momentarily robbed of the wind, for an instant were alone to be heard. "Ready! 'Bout ship!" shouted Nalley. Flap, flap, went the canvass; the cordage rattled through the pulleys; the great boom swung over to starboard. The Widgeon paused, staggered for a moment, like a racer catching for breath, then glided on across the crystal eddying wake of the brig, upon whose stern the words "Halcyon, of G——," were yet indistinctly legible, and in another moment both vessels were side by side, heading towards home.

"They are all talking to the pilot, asking him the news," said Nalley, turning to the major. Kate, one hand upon her father's shoulder, her ringlets fluttering in the breeze, her eyes radiant, her face flushed, was leaning forward, watching with unspeakable earnestness the scene on the deck above them.

The major said " Speak them, Nalley."

" Halcyon, ahoy, there," shouted the pilot.

" Don't want any pilot—got one, don't you see," said a tall, raw-boned man, leaning both hands on the taffrail, then pointing aloft.

" Are you the captain ?" asked Nalley.

" Yes, sir."

" How many passengers ?"

" One." Kate gave a faint cry.

" Name ?"

"*Sherburne.*"

These words brought a shudder to the major, while Kate sank weeping upon the bench.

" Reported you had three shipwrecked people."

" Had two," answered the captain. " Other was a lady; both lost on the Erebus." The major started.

" Where is "—Nalley's arm was grasped.

" Don't—oh—don't ask him." said Kate. " Oh God —how can we bear this answer ?"

The major put his arm about her, and folded her to his heart, as if to shield her from all evil. " Be brave, my child," he said, "we must know all sooner or later. Nalley, ask him who was his other passenger."

The rawboned skipper appeared to grow impatient. "Lady passengers a heap of trouble. Anxious to get home. Transferred her to a New York steamer two days ago. Must be there by this time."

"Her name?" asked Nalley now himself all emotion.

"*Loring*," shouted the captain, turning away. Nalley turned his eyes, wet with tears of excitement and joy. Near him on the deck, with up-turned eyes, knelt the gray haired husband, the sunny-haired daugher, forgetful of all save their gratitude for that great and unlooked-for deliverance.

VI.

Jack Sparrow's coming birthday party vied with the Goodstone races in exciting the joyous anticipations of the younger population of G——. Jack Sparrow, everybody knew. He was a good-hearted, whole-souled young fellow. He never saw a child crying in the streets without stopping to ask the reason, and, if possible, alleviate its bitter grief. He did not grind down into the earth with his passing heel the marbles of small boys playing on the sidewalks or in the squares. He never had been known to do a mean or ungentlemanly act to anybody, rich or poor. Tom Sparrow was proud of his boy, and with good cause, for everyone liked him and promised well for him in the future.

He had come home from his second term Sophomore at Y—— to celebrate a birthday, which came in the college holidays, fortunately. Now, on his arrival, he found that invitations had been issued, and that scores upon scores of his acquaintances, intimate and otherwise, were to celebrate with him, in his father's parlors, his completion of eighteen years' existence in this transitory world.

He found the house topsey-turvey with preparation. His indulgent paternal relative, whose pleadings he had, when a boy and taken to court by his father to keep him out of mischief at home, listened to with respectful awe, he saw divested of his professional dignity, dancing about the house in a high state of expectant activity. He found his affectionate mother who called him "dear little boy" to this day, too busy to ask him all the news of his absence. He concluded to surrender at discretion, and to appear in the character of host in a style commensurate with the preparations.

Tom Sparrow came home rather puzzled from his interview at the hotel. "Very strange, wife," said he. "Did you read the Gazette this morning?"

"Now don't you know, Tom, I havn't even had time to eat a mouthful of dinner."

"Yes, yes, I remember," said Tom, dancing out of the way of a servant bouncing in with a waiter full of glassware. "Something very funny, though. Loring's gone out into the harbor to meet a brig on which he thinks his wife is."

"Why, he is a widower, I thought."

"That's just what he thought himself," said the little man, roguishly, "until he saw the paper this morning, reporting the safety of three survivors of a shipwreck where his wife was supposed to have been lost. Can't I persuade you, my dear Mrs. S., to take an ocean voyage with me?"

"Now, Tom, don't joke on such subjects, I beg of you. And so, Major Loring is in this terrible suspense. I pray that she may be restored to him. What would be my feelings, you dear old fellow, if I were sailing back to you after you thought me dead?"

"And mine, Molly (he always called her Molly in extremely affectionate moments), if I were expecting you?"

"How Jack would laugh," she said, "to hear us talking so. But now, while I think of it, I want you to go to the depot to-morrow morning and see about that fruit and wine, Parmelee was to send me up from New York. Don't forget it."

Precisely twenty-four hours after Major Loring and Kate had reached G——, the Express train came dashing in again, and its passengers came pouring out upon the platform, where, among others, stood dapper Tom Sparrow waiting the new arrivals.

He saw the passengers come pouring out, men, women and children—homely and handsome, rich and poor—all in the American hurry to get to their destinations as expeditiously as possible. He saw the baggage-men and drivers rushing hither and thither, beckoning to this one, speaking to that one, jostling everybody. He saw the passengers who only alighted for breakfast at the eating-saloon hurrying in to swallow a cup of coffee and a piece of railway beefsteak, as if their lives depended on a combination of speed and voracity. He saw the cases of wine and the box of fruit bearing his address deposited in the express wagon, and was turning to go when he heard a female voice inquiring:

"Is there a gentleman by the name of Major Loring at the Wilton House, do you know?"

The question was addressed to the hotel baggage-man, who, with a huge trunk on his shoulder, was, with unsteady step, moving towards his wagon.

"Major Loring?—yes, ma'am; him and daughter arrived yesterday; took their baggage up; stopping at room 24. Kerridge, ma'am?"

"Thank you; I shall be obliged if you will call one for me."

Sparrow looked closely at her whose inquiry for his friend had attracted his attention. He saw a matron lady of prepossessing appearance, dressed in black and veiled, yet not sufficiently to conceal a countenance both refined and benevolent in its expression. A momentary thought flashed over him—"No," he said, "it can't be—the Halcyon came in last night. But I'll offer my assistance at all events."

So the little man smoothed his coat, pulled up his collar, gave a glance downward at his general external appearance, and then, taking off his hat, bowed most politely to the lady, saying: "Madame, pardon this liberty. I heard you inquire concerning Major Loring, did I not? I am an intimate acquaintance of his," and, with another bow, he handed his card, upon which she read:

> Thomas Sparrow,
> Attorney and Counsellor.

"He is stopping at the Wilton House, madame, and if you will allow, I shall take pleasure in conducting you to him and his daughter."

The lady, thus unexpectedly addressed, appeared for a moment undecided how to reply.

"Are they well?" she asked in tremulous voice.

"Perfectly," said Sparrow; "I left them yesterday about to sail down the harbor to meet a vessel coming in from Calcutta. They must have returned before midnight, for the Halcyon is here."

"Is here?" said the lady starting. "I beg you, without delay, conduct me to Major and Miss Loring's hotel."

"Here's your Kerridge, ma'am," said the baggage-man, returning quite out of breath.

"Madame," said Sparrow, bowing most respectfully, "we lawyers are curious. May I be permitted, as a friend of Major Loring's, to ask a single question; to ask if you are"—

"His wife, sir," replied Mrs. Loring, "so long separated from him, and so soon, I trust, to be restored to him."

Sparrow, no longer in cautious doubt, fairly danced with glee. "Why, my dear madame, I cannot express my happiness. When I left your anxious husband and daughter yesterday they knew not whether to rejoice in hope or be patient in tribulation. Imagine their suspense. They knew that survivors of the ship on which you all were wrecked, were coming by the Halcyon. They knew nothing more, and 'twixt hope and doubt they sailed down to meet the expected vessel. But what must have been their agony of disappointment? You arrive by the train. I'm puzzled, madame, I'm puzzled in the midst of my happiness."

"I was transferred at sea from the Halcyon to a New York bound steamer, which reached there yesterday," said Mrs. Loring, the tears coming into her eyes, after hearing Sparrow's recital. "I beg you sir, do not detain me longer from them. The carriage is waiting."

Sparrow saw her to the carriage door. "I would that it were in my power to persuade you, madame, to defer the reunion until I shall have paved the way by an interview with your husband and daughter. I am apprehensive that, disappointed as they must be by the events of yesterday, the sudden revulsion of feeling certain to ensue from your entrance unannounced might be of serious injury to both you and your daughter—perhaps even to our dear old major himself—schooled as he is to self-control."

"This had not occurred to me," she said, "but what do you propose sir?"

"That my wife, Mrs. Sparrow, who, yesterday, by the way, met your husband, be, for a few hours, your hostess, while I, meanwhile, go and break the news."

She looked closely into his face—travel and society, and reading, had combined to make her a physiognomist—she judged the little man aright, when she read in his good natured countenance, when he made the proposition, nothing but the promptings of a kindly heart.

"You are very generous and considerate, sir," she replied, "let it be as you say; but you can imagine the struggle which the delayed reunion costs me."

"The down train leaves at ten o'clock, this morning, papa," said Kate, sitting by their hotel parlor window with the paper in her hand. "We have little time to lose. See, it is nine, already."

The room was divested of that cheery home-like aspect which Kate, after unpacking the trunks, had given it on the previous day. It had resumed the appearance it had presented when they first entered it yesterday morning, and near the doorway the trunks were strapped and ready for the expressman.

"We must not miss it under any circumstances, papa," Kate continued. "Did you send the dispatch to Uncle Matt?"

"Just as you wrote it, dear," he answered. "I do believe I have lost my self-possession for once, Kate. Where is my cigar-case?"

Rat-tat-tat. There came a lively rap on the door, and Sparrow's face, rosier than its wont, was thrust in. "Good morning, good morning," said he—"why, what's the meaning of these trunks, Loring? Are they yours, or did they come on the Halcyon?"

"Tom," said the major, "we are off post haste for New York by this morning's train. This dear girl's mother, my wife, is saved—is, even now without doubt, awaiting us there. I have sent a dispatch that we are coming at once."

Sparrow, for once, feigned delight and surprise, but whistled in his sleeve at the dilemma. "And how did you learn this?" he asked.

"The captain of the Halcyon told us," said Kate. "He has been here this morning to tell us all about mamma. She was transferred at sea to a New York bound steamer."

Sparrow was nonplussed. "The train goes at ten," he said; "you've got plenty of time to stop and say good-bye to Mrs. Sparrow on your way to the depot. In your suspense and anxiety, that will be an excellent plan for killing off the intervening three-quarters of an hour—what say you?"

"Yes, papa," said Kate. "Mr. Sparrow has been so kind and attentive that—

"No, no—not I," said Sparrow. "Come—I want my wife to, at least, have an opportunity of seeing you, Miss Kate, before your unexpectedly sudden departure."

The major, acquiescing in his daughter's request, the carriage was called. When the baggage-man came in, Sparrow slipped a quarter in his hand and whispered, "Don't mention that lady at the depot." The fellow knew his business and kept still.

Through the shaded streets they drove rapidly to Sparrow's house. As they neared it, the little man felt that he must give his companions an inkling of what was to come.

"Loring," said he, "I'd be willing to wager a basket of Green Seal that you won't catch that train."

"We have'nt much time to lose, I know," said the

major—"we'll just wish Mrs. Sparrow good-morning and be obliged to make our adieus in the same breath. The train must not be missed."

"I'd wager another basket of Clicquot that if the train came in an hour behind time you would'nt catch it," continued Sparrow, with a mischievous look in his eye and a smile lurking about his lips, as he looked from Kate to her father, as if to detect suspicion of his intent.

Kate, with a woman's instinct did suspect.

"I don't understand what you can foresee to detain us," she said quickly.

"Something," he said, still mischievously, still archly smiling.

"Tom, you are as inveterate a joker as ever you were, I see," said the major; "I'll be bound a pun is coming."

"No—no pun this time, Loring; better than that, old fellow: somebody—"

"Who?" they both asked in a breath.

"Can't you imagine?" he asked.

"It can't be poss—oh! papa, papa—see there—there at the window," cried Kate, clapping her hands and pointing toward the house before which the carriage had stopped—"oh, dear, darling mamma! yes, we're coming —quick driver—quick, please."

A glance sufficed the gray-haired major. In it he saw the dear face he had believed he would never look upon again; in it he saw, full of love, tearful eyes gazing fondly into his.

"Coming, dear wife, coming," he said, as she hastened to meet him.

> All was ended now—the hope and the fear and the anguish,
> All the aching of heart, the restless, unsatisfied longing,
> All the dull, deep pain and constant anguish of patience;

and in another moment their outstretched arms were locked about each other's necks, two loving, trusting souls reposed upon the dear old soldier's bosom, and two fond faces looked tearfully up into his as he lifted up his eyes and murmured, "Father, we thank Thee."

Jack Sparrow's birthday party came off that night in glorious style. The parlors were brilliant with gaslight, beauty and wit. Sparrow, *pater*, was everywhere among the guests, quite wild with excitement, and making visits to the wine table in the dining-room so frequently as to occasion a gentle admonition from the vigilant Mrs. S——. Jack did the honors of host with an éclat truly admirable, and was quietly voted a charming young man and a superb dancer by every young lady in the room, not excepting those pretty school girls who had pinched the stupid professor. But it was not until, weary with the dance, the happy assemblage gathered about the supper table, that rosy Tom Sparrow, in his jolly good nature a very Bacchus incarnate, rose, and filling his glass to the brim, rapped for silence, and said, " You all must have heard of the happy reunion which transpired under this roof to-day. Ladies and gentleman, fill your glasses. I propose a toast: THE HALCYON'S RETURN!"

SUB ULMIS.

Under the elms we walked
   As the moon was climbing the sky,
And vowed, as we tenderly talked,
   Together to live and to die.

How little, how little we thought,
   When living those moments of bliss,
That hard-hearted time could have brought
   Such cold separation as this.

And yet—was there not in each heart
   A vague apprehension; a dread
That after all this, we might part
   And be to each other as dead?

Ah yes! for it was but a dream,
   A sunset that sinks in the sea,
A waif floating down on life's stream.
   For now she is dead unto me.

Under the elms I walk
   As the moon is climbing the sky,
And vow, as unanswered I talk,
   That alone I will live and will die.

MY CASTLES.

Domes and minarets and towers—
   Turrets which can kiss the sky,
Grottoes cool, and leafy bowers
   Clad in buds that never die,
These, and beauties twice as fair,
Deck my castles in the air.

Flecks of clouds, all bright and golden,
   Hover round their shadowy walls;
Strains and voices, sweet and olden,
   Echo through those spectral halls.
Many an angel lingers where
Float my castles in the air.

Oft at sunset as I ponder
   O'er the glories in the West,
And my restless spirits wander
   Far and wide in search of rest,
Angels whisper "See, 'tis there,
   In yon castles in the air."

But when I approach them nearer,
   And their beauties fain would clasp,
Neither more distinct nor clearer,
   Ever they elude my grasp.
And I turn in sad despair
From my castles in the air.

THE VOUDOUX AND THEIR CHARMS.

Eight or ten squares back from St. C—— Street, running parallel thereto, is a street known as V—— Street, a quiet thoroughfare, where people may live all the year round without encountering any greater excitement than that caused by the running away of a grocer's horse or the arrest of a mid-night brawler. Pleasant rows of cottages front upon its sidewalks, lines of shade trees are growing before them, and in the evening scores upon scores of happy children romp until bed-time. In short, V—— Street is quiet, retired, and usually devoid of great events.

But one morning last week there came a sensation. The dwellers in one of those quiet houses were astonished, perhaps somewhat unpleasantly so, to find upon their doorstep, not the traditional basket and baby, not an anonymous letter, or warning from the Ku-klux, but, more strange than either, the quivering heart of a beef, stuffed with tacks and wild herbs, and wrapped around with black crape.

Now, in any other city save this, such a discovery would suggest no more than the trick of a mischievous boy, and the finders would throw away the nonsensical

THE VOUDOUX AND THEIR CHARMS. 59

trash, and think no more of it. But in this case notice was immediately sent to the Lieutenant of Police, and steps were taken to have the author of the mystery apprehended. However impotent and silly may be the means, the leaving of this strange charm had a meaning; one which, had it been left at the door of some of the negroes living in this great city would have terrified them almost into their graves; but which, in the present case, being conveyed to white persons of intelligence, and devoid of superstition, only marks them as the silent objects of some ignorant person's hatred.

In other words, this was the work of the Voudoux, whose creed is an old relic of African superstition, made up of incantations, conjuror's arts and savage rites, which even to this day finds its votaries in this city. Threaten a negro with the curse of the Voudou Queen, and you invoke upon him or her all the terrors of the Inferno. An inexplicable horror seizes upon the one thus threatened, and the only preservative is in counter charms. Many and many a time have servants, under supposed indignities from their employers, gone to consult with "the Queen," generally a withered old crone, dressed in black, head-handkerchief and all, who, for a fee, gives the incensed one advice, whether pacificatory or the contrary. The writer remembers a case where a mulatto servant girl, while opening some feather pillows, found a number of little knots, or balls, into which, as is generally the case, the feathers had by long use shaped themselves. Immediately she burst into a fit of loud crying, and calling her mistress, showed her the knots in question. Nothing could quiet her or induce her to touch the pillows or feathers again. It was a Voudou charm, she said, foretelling no good to those who slept upon the pillow. In vain it was attempted to explain to her excited comprehension that electricity had caused the conglomeration of the feathers. Straightway she proceeded to consult the nearest Voudou Queen. Royalty received her with due ceremony, and having heard the story of the pillows, said that it had indeed been a charm wrought for some body, but not for those who then nightly laid their heads to rest upon it. And so the woman was quieted, but she never fully recovered from the shock.

Now and then, the police discover votaries of Voudouism in their orgies, dancing naked about a cauldron, uttering terrific yells, in fact carrying out to the letter, one of those savage scenes which travelers have told us are occasionally to be witnessed among the tribes of the interior of Africa. By the indescribable terror and imaginary power with which these "Queens" thus invest themselves, do they obtain this influence over their votaries. There is one "Doctor John" who is said to possess healing power to a miraculous extent. And lately, too, a valuable lot of stolen diamonds are said to have been reclaimed through the directions given by a Voudou.

So it came that when one morning the inmates of the quiet house on V—— Street found on their doorstep, the beef's heart served up in green herbs, tacks and crape, they felt themselves fully justified in informing the police that some unknown person was thus manifesting a feeling of hostility toward them.

"MERRY CHRISTMAS."—There is an old tradition, and a beautiful one it is, that during these winter nights in the Christmas holidays, spirits and faries are abroad in the air, flitting here and there in the starlight, wafting happiness and good cheer down upon the sleeping world. Children smile in their dreams, and over old brows weary with the toil of life, come in for a brief moment, a brighter vision. The season upon which we are just entering is consecrated to mirth, to peace, to good will toward all. If it finds us unhappy, it will drive away our griefs; while on the other hand it cannot but intensify the joys of a happy heart. So, let us forget trouble for awhile, and put away from our thoughts all that would remind us of life's burdens. Let us give ourselves up to the happiness of the season while we may. There is enough beyond; when it comes meet it, but let the morrow take thought for the things of itself.

THE CARPET-BAGGER'S SOLILOQUY.

To starve or not to starve; that's what's the matter.
Whether 'tis better for a while to suffer
The pangs and growlings of a hungry stomach,
Or take up arms against Democracy,
And by it make a living. To eat; to starve
No more, and by a good square meal to end
The stomach-ache, and all the thousand woes
Poor men are heir to; 'tis a consummation
Devoutly to be wished. To eat—to feed.
To drink—perchance get tight—aye, that's the talk,
For in those drunken hours what plans may come!
Then I'll have shuffled off these shabby clothes
And rigged anew. In this respect
I never was so seedy in my life.
Who wouldn't bear the hoots and jeers of boys,
The look of scorn, the proud man's contumely,
The pangs of despised love, the law's delay,
The insolence of office, and the spurns
That loyal merit of the unpardoned takes,
When he himself may his own fortune make
By turning Rad? Who a valise would bear,
To grunt and sweat beneath the weary load,
But that the hope of something afterward,
A seat in the Convention out of which
No member goes home poor—sustains the will
And makes one glad to tote his carpet bag
And mix with people that he knows not of.
And thus the darkened hue of legislation
Is sicklied o'er with the pale caste, I've thought,
And enterprises of great pith and moment
With this regard their currents turn awry
And lose the name of action.

AN AUDIENCE IN THE DARK.

Reader, have you ever been attacked by Phantasmagoria? If you haven't, we have, and can recommend the complaint as an admirable dispeller of the blues. The symptoms came on last evening, as, entering the C—— Place Baptist Church, we found there collected a goodly number of people, most of them young people, all anticipating an attack similar to that which threatened ourselves. In the chancel there had been erected a white screen, and, looking toward this, some indefinable misgiving crossed our mind. But casting aside these foolish fears, and sinking quietly down into a velvet cushioned pew, we resigned ourselves to the attack.

It came on as dreamily and pleasantly as the effects of a narcotic gently stealing over the senses, and soothing them to rest. First came music, "Flee as a Bird unto the Mountains," sung by a quintette, with piano accompaniment, and sung very charmingly, too. Then, of a sudden, out went the lights. Aha, we thought, now the Phantasmagoria come on apace. Light after light, to the very last one, was extinguished, and lo! the whole interior of the church was in utter darkness. Whether or not young couples managed to carry on their conversation under such adverse circumstances; whether diffident swains were emboldened by their invisibility to say what, in the light, they would never have ventured upon; whether others, anxious to clear themselves from all suspicions, sat bolt upright out of reach of anybody, we can't say, but we do know that when the black darkness came, young babies began to expostulate with their mammas, and hilarious boys about the outskirts of the assemblage, made bold to applaud, especially when, upon the white screen, there appeared in rapid succession a series of illuminated pictures, representing scriptural scenes, such as the Good Samaritan, the Virgin Mary and her child, and various others. Each of these the boys welcomed with that prolonged, hushed, "Oh-h-h," indicative of most intense boyish satisfaction, while the older folks looked on evidently equally, though less demonstratively, appreciative. Once in a while, when the reflection was dim, the boys would cry "More light," which praiseworthy desire was promptly gratified by the doubly invisible manager behind the screen.

In the basement of the church three or four beautifully decorated tables had been spread with an abundance of delicacies, and hither, after the exhibition above had concluded, the assemblage adjourned. We were obliged to bid farewell to the pleasant scene, some time before the entertainment ended, but left with memories of a warm hospitality, and with the assurance that an attack of Phantasmagoria is by no means so deplorable an occurrence as one ignorant of its nature might imagine.

Oh! Perfectly Sober.—An application was made a few nights ago to the superintendent of police to release a man who had been locked up for intoxication, the applicant offering to give bonds for the delinquent's appearance on the following day. "Bring him in, and let's see his condition," said the superintendent, temporarily turning away to attend to some other business, while the friend, accompanied by a special, went to bring in the incarcerated for inspection. Ten minutes later, a terrible racket in the hall was audible; shuffling of feet, stamping and shouting, all combined to astonish the occupants of the superintendent's office. The door flew open, and lo! a tableau was presented. Propped up in the arms of the special officer on one side, and the applicant for his release on the other, affectionately leaned the inebriate, his knees doubled up under him, his chin in his vest, hat banged in, eyes half open, and arms hanging limp and lifeless. "Is this the man you want me to release as sober?" inquired the superintendent. "Wake up Tom," said the friend, slily kicking the drunkard; "wake up my boy." "Go tell," groaned the bacchanal, opening his eyes for a moment, and lunging backward in an effort to sprawl on the floor. It was too much for the superintendent. "Oh, take him back where he came from," he said impatiently, and the curtain fell.

TO A CHILD WAKING FROM SLEEP.

"And where have you been, my darling?
 And why do your great blue eyes
Look wond'ringly round on all things,
 As if in a strange surprise?"

Ah! could she but speak, we should hear her say:
"I've wandered in dreamland, so far away,
I'd nigh forgotten this mortal earth,
And the doting mother who gave me birth.
But your sweet caresses recall me now,
As I feel your lips on my childish brow,
As your tender hands through my ringlets creep.
 Mother, I only have been asleep.

"And what have you seen, my darling,
 What visions of sunny skies
Have flitted athwart your soul, that now
 They shine in your waking eyes?"

"Oh! mother, I've been where the roses bloom,
And violets scatter their sweet perfume,
Where sunbeams linger from morn till night,
'Till the fruit grows ripe in their mellow light.
Where gentlest of fragrant zephyrs blow,
Where the wild bird's warbling is soft and low,
Where clearest streamlets murmuring leap.
 Mother, I only have been asleep.

"And who have you met, my darling?
 What beauteous forms were they
That left their semblance upon your brow
 In your journey so far away?

"I wandered dear mother, with cherubs there
Whose laughing eyes, and whose golden hair,
Were fairer far than I e'er can tell,
And their angel radiance on me fell
As we wandered together, hand in hand,
Through flowers and sunlight, a happy band ;
Such bright companions I fain would keep,
    But mother, I only have been asleep.

"May it ever be thus, my darling,
    May those wee little hands and feet
Ne'er find companions less cheery,
    . Or wander 'mid flowers less sweet."

AN ACROSTIC.

FROM A CHILD TO SANTA CLAUS.

Say, Santa Claus—my pa has told me
A funny story of yourself ;
Now tell me this, I pray don't scold me!
Tell me—are you a tiny elf,
An ugly monster, or a jolly,
Corpulent, little red-faced fellow?
Let me know! pray forgive my folly,
Are you white, black, blue, brown or yellow ?
Upon my little knees I pray—
Say, Santa Claus, who are you? say.

SOPHRONISSIMA; OR, THE VAGROM'S COMPREHENSION.

I.

'Twas dewy morn. A gallant youth of twenty-two springs might have been seen by his landlady or washerwoman (nobody else cared to see him) passing with melancholy gait along the magnificent Roo de Poydras 'Twas Gustavus Alphonso. Reared from an infancy in which poor and honest parents had exhausted upon him their fullest muscular abilities, he had at the romantic age of ten, voluntarily sought the paths of music and literature, by vending song books. Sweet child! Casting aside the trammels of an obscure birth, he had pressed onward and upward, ever aspiring, ever inscribing "Excelsior" upon his victorious banners, until we find fortune smiling upon his efforts and rewarding his genius with the responsible position of second clerk of a peanut stand. "Ha-ha!" had he exclaimed on the day the office was tendered him. "Now indeed this cold, artless wor-r-rld shall know Gustavus Alphonso.

Did I say that, on this dewy morn, he was melancholy? I did, and I repeat it. He owed money to his landlady, residing in a palatial mansion on Corduroy Alley. He had guv her his note, and just as sure as the dew fell that morning, that morning the note fell due. "Heavings!" he exclaimed; "can this be what the poets call grief?

Why these brains to feel—these hearts to think? Alas! for my impetuous impecuniosity—it is, it is."

He entered the Poydrassian Market. Seating his aristocratic figure upon a stool before a coffee stand, "What ho, Giovanni," he cried, "come hither, thou degenerate descendant of the Latin kings, and bring me in thy dainty digits a steaming cup of aromatic Mocha."

'Twas brought, aye, brought. He sipped, he drank, and with the beverage his soul did warm. Throwing down a dime, his very last, with easy grace upon the counter, "Take thy gold, tradesman," he shouted; "and now—and now—relentless landlady, inexorable dame, widow of the lamented Pat McFudge (whose nose was bit off on the levee some years ago, from which he died of it), now, remorseless female, I go to meet thee, Aha, aha!"

(If dramatized, use blue lights at this juncture.)

II.

The widow McFudge was a gentle creature of two hundred and ten pounds weight. Her nose brightly beamed upon all who enquired the price of board and apartments in her two-story brick caravansera, in the precincts of the boulevard Corduroy. She kept her house thoroughly upon the you-rope-in-style; every one could order what he liked—and if he didn't get it went without—the house in a hurry.

Now and then the amiability of the fair hostess and her delicate health combined to induce her to indulge in artificial stimulants. Upon such occasions, the care of the establishment devolved upon her orfling niece, Sopronissima Snoozewell, a gushing young maiden of thirty-one. In such a moment, when serving him with hash one morning at breakfast, had she won the love of Gustavus Alphonso. "Soffy," he had said in endearing terms, "Soffy dear, accept the 'art of an unappreciated child of genius. Tergether we'll soar to the peaks of the Halps, or like Claude Duval—no! Melnotte, and his Pauleen—we'll seek some quiet spot, and live there for some years. Oh, heavings, Soffy, why answers thou not me frantic prayer?"

"Yes, but whose a goin to pay expenses there and back?" had answered Sopronissima inquiringly, a thoughtful hesitation upon her classic brow, as she poured hot water into the tea-pot.

"Me—me—your own Gustavus Alphonso."

"Then thou art yours or I am mine forever," she had replied and fainted, her head falling into the butter dish.

"And now," murmured Gustavus, "now for—for—for —some hash."

III.

But to return from our transgression. The mellifluous orb of day (otherwise known as old Sol) was diffusing his incandescent beams about twenty minutes of nine on the eventful morning upon which our story opens, when the doors of the McFudge House were burst rudely open, and Gustavus Alphonso entered, his eyes rolling in fine poetic frenzy, crying aloud, "Where is she? I must see her. Conduct me to her immejitly." Some ladies of the neighborhood, who had called in to take their morning glass of whisky with the amiable widow McFudge, knocked the ashes from their clay pipes, and said " Who is this gentleman?"

"A child of genius, ladies," he answered, "seeking her who would devour him. Can'st tell me where is Lady McFudge?"

"I am here," shouted a stentorian voice. "Behold your injured landlady."

(N. B.—This was true; she had fell down the back stairs the night before and injured herself considerable.)

Around him Gustavus Alponso drew his coat; from his pocket drew a thousand dollars. "Name my diabolical liabilities, madam," said he, in fiercest tones. "Them notes, them notes, projuce them."

She did.

"I pay thee this; here take thy money," shrieked Alphonso, tearing the notes into a million pieces, and staggering to the kitchen door where he trod upon the tail of Soffy's pet tom-cat, which he set up a howling and brought his fair young mistress to the scene.

Her hair was in curl papers.

"Aha, false one, I know thee now. The ball! this night! thy hair curling! I see—I see it all; and now me cry is vengence!"

The ladies by the fire-place stood aghast. Soffy burst into tears. "I don't know nothin' about you," she said, "away wicked man; depart, receiver of young female hearts; reducer of virtuous beauty. Thy fiendish charms can't no longer ensnare me soul. Away! Away!"

"Beware, young woming," screamed Alphonso shaking a fifty before her astonished vision, "thou'st rashly, recklessly risked relentless revenge. I go. I go! But thou shall hear from Gustavus Alphonso."

She saw the magic flutter of the greenback. It stole over her (five) senses, as the gushing tones of a hand organ over a slumbering colored person. "Come back," she cried in accents wild, "Gustavus, oh Gustavus." But not seeing him return after a reasonable time, fainted.

IV.

Them people who are unacquainted with the use of money, knows generally nothing of the use of it. Shakspeare and the other historians tells us that money is a good thing to have about the house, and it therefore becomes necessary to relate how the hero of this pretty little tale come by the money in question, which he paid his bill with it, and shook a fifty in the false fair's face. But why dilate? Rushing forth that morning from the market he had encountered a noble colored man, who was running for Kongress, and who had drawn his bounty money from the freedman's bureau.

"Come hither, son of Afric," said he, in ke-indest tones, "dost know me?"

"Don' 'no nuffin' 'bout ye," was the haughty reply.

"I am the benefactor of thy race—I am Phillips."

"Ha! is you Wennel Phillips, uh?"

"'Tis he. I come to relieve you of all the burdens which fill your heart (and pocket)."

Suffice it to say, that in the brief space of fifteen minutes, gentle reader, the relief came, and Gustavus soared on love's pinions toward his Soffy's abode.

But now he had found she was false to him, *Alas! Alas!*

V.

'Twas a sweet night in July, the soft hum of the whipperwill, mingled with the odor of the night blooming cereus, came born upon the noctuous air as two lovers clinging tenderly to each other's arms wandered carelessly through the broken railing of L—— Square, and seated themselves upon one of the elaborately carved iron sofas which a beneficent city had provided for their entertainment.

She was lovely. The beauty of her regular Grecian face was marred by no Grecian bend. She wore a Swiss tulle, trimmed with mauve brocade and ornamented with pompadours de chambrey. Upon her head, shrouding her features, was a blue cotton veil. Who was this elegant creature?" She twirled her kid glove (size 8) quite mournfully in her left hand. Heavings, 'twas Sophronissima.

Strange as this may seem, disgusted though indulgent reader, 'twas indeed she. But a stranger was the man who was with her this balmy night. Was it Gustavus? you ask with a shudder. It was not—alas—alas.

The music and merry feet were issuing from the windows of an opposite Hall, for there was a ball there, and Soffy was goin', but had just stepped into the square to compose herself. *He had proposed.*

Ah! what bliss. This gentle stranger had come to Mrs. McFudge's that morning to take refuge from a heartless policeman who had sought to arrest him for picking pockets. Sophronissima's eyes had lit upon his manly frame. " 'Twas enuff," she said, " ajoo, Gustavus ; 'enceforth me 'art is another's." And to Rodolphus she had blighted her vowels.

But as they sat there a dark form lurked behind a circumjacent tree; and a sound as of crackling peanuts at the theatre, might have been heard. Soffy started. "Methought," she said, "I erd the voice of one who is me enemy."

"Do but show me the traitor," muttered Rodolphus,

and his countenance is doomed to disfigurement, his eyes to mayhem, his nose and ear to the impress of my murderous rodents."

The dark form approached, and nearer came the terrific crash of peanuts. It stood before them.

" 'Tis then thus thou," it said, and throwing back a heavy cloak of dark velvet disclosed the plowed and harrowed liniments of Gustavus.

"Further disguise is useless," he shrieked, and now for war."

Rodolphus caught the fainting, screaming lady in his arms, and gently deposited her sinking form on the grass. "What sayst thou, base hireling? Who art thou?"

"Aha, sirrah, thy foe Gustavus Alphonso. This card will tell thee all. Here," and he handed his card.

"I know thee not, but I will mur-r-rder-r-r thee," shouted Rodolphus.

"Come on traitor, I defy thee."

Soffy come to, right away. "Off, deceiver," she screamed, "nor molest my angelic Rodolphus."

"And thou," uttered Alphonso, in accents wild, tearing the chignon from her classic head, "get thee off, for the battle is nigh."

And so was the policeman—inexorable justice, whether coming in the form of a special officer or a bench warrant —which the policeman seized Rodolphus.

But our story has gone too far. 'Tis well, 'tis well.

OVER THE SEAS.

Here, as I sit on the sands,
Looking far over the sparkling sea,
Dancing and rippling in merry glee,
Beauteous and bright are the visions I see;
   Visions of sunny and distant lands
My wandering fancy brings to me.

Visions of waving palms
Nodding their tops to the spicy breeze,
As it lullingly whispers amid the trees,
Greet me from over the laughing seas;
   Zephyrs laden with fragrant balms,
And dreamy odors which soothe and please.

Crystal and azure lakes,
Scattered as stars o'er the sky at night,
Glitt'ring like gems thro' the landscape bright,
Hills with their summits bathed in light,
   And snow-clad beauty which ne'er forsakes
The shadowy top of each cloud-capped height.

Maidens with laughing eyes,
Gathering flowers, thro' the meadows rove,
Or, crowned with wreaths which their fair hands wove,
Sport with wild mirth in each shady grove;
   And then as each wreath of flow'rets dies,
They smile, and call it a type of love.

Thus, as I sit on the sands,
Visions of beauty around me play,
Clad in the haze of this summer's day,
Pausing awhile on their shadowy way;
   And I look and long for those distant lands,
Smiling and sunny and far away.

A LOUISIANA BAYOU SCENE.

Rumors came that in a dull, sluggish bayou, flowing through cypress swamps and willow groves, not ten miles away, there was to be had an abundance of perch and pike, such as even the venerable Izaak might not have despised. Accordingly, behold a party of four of us, at sunrise, taking the ferry-boat at the stock-landing and crossing to Gretna, on the opposite side of the river. Baskets of provisions and tackle, tapering bamboo poles, and the indispensable black bottle, make up the equipments. The ferry-boat puffs and snorts as the rapid current carries her some distance below the point where she would be. The engineer is at his post; above the door of his engine-room a sign, "No admittance except on biz."

We land and meet half a score of half-naked young negroes, of ages varying from sixteen to twenty, each demanding, in no gentle tone, "Have a tow, sir?" "Want a boat?" We single out one of these, remarkable chiefly for his breadth of mouth, and, replying affirmatively, are conducted to the head of Harvey's Canal, two hundred yards distant, only separated by the high levee bank from the river. It is a narrow strip of water running directly back from the river, extending like a silver band as far as the eye reaches, and fringed on either side with a luxuriant verdure. It was dug some twenty-five years since by him whose name it bears, and who now resides hard by, in a mansion, and upon an estate, of princely elegance, its object being to open direct communication with Barrataria Bay from the river, through a bayou into which the canal empties at a distance of six miles from the Mississippi. But unfortunately, the proprietor has never yet obtained from the authorities permission to construct a lock at the head of the canal, through which boats may enter from the river, and, as a consequence, the enterprise, though within an inch of its completion, remains to be used as a very convenient highway for the inhabitants of the back country, and for those who, like the writer, would pass through it to the sport beyond.

A number of skiffs are moored here, and into one of these we step, carefully, even tenderly, depositing the baskets where sun and moisture cannot reach them. A short distance off, the Opelousas Railroad bridge crosses, and, as we pull under its shadow, we inwardly hope there may be no passing train to rattle the dust into our eyes. Now the oars are shipped, and the broad-mouthed Ethiopian, mounted upon a lazy mule, throws us a long line, one end of which is fastened to his saddle, while the other we make fast to our light little craft. The mule breaks off into a sleepy jog (the tow path here is twenty feet above our heads,) and we shoot off, the water rippling noisily away from under the bow. Ah! this is glorious laziness, and our Jehu above there drives his heels into the mule's sides, guffawing from glee as he goes. It is only seven o'clock in the morning (how sound asleep we usually are at this hour,) and the unwonted exercise has given an appetite which suggests breakfast time. So the baskets are opened, and from their recesses come ham sandwiches, soft shell crabs, and many other dainties which the forethought of those dear ones at home has provided.

Now and then, upon the banks we see grouped two or three of the newly-enfranchised, reveling in the luxuries incidental to landing their favorite catfish. The bank gradually becomes lower as we progress, and is now but a foot above the level of the water. Blackberry bushes, brilliant with their ripening fruit, line the canal on either side, willow and cypress and pine trees are in the background, while, under the shade of overhanging grass on the margin, crocuses and lilies hide their modest heads. In the water, minnows dart hither and thither in thousands, a wily moccasin, now and then, stops in his transit to watch us, and the great gar-fish leaps up ahead, splashing the water into a foam with his black finny back.

Now the tow-path ends, and our mule and driver go galloping back to the starting point, with instructions to report at four o'clock. Now we take to the oars again; a mile or two more, traveled in snailish contrast with our previous rate of locomotion, bring us to Bayou St. John, or Bayou Barrataria (either name will do) into which, crossing the line of the canal at right-angles, we emerge as from a narrow lane upon a broad highway. Now we are near the waters made historical by the adventures of the pirate Lafitte; here it was that, weary of the seas, he and his companion-freebooters in the ancient French and Spanish territorial days repaired to rest for a while from the chase for booty, and count and secrete their treasures. Half a dozen old hulks and barges lie moored or sunken at the mouth of the canal, and, further to the left, lies a little steamer, old-fashioned and dismantled. In front frowns a thick forest of moss-covered pines, with an undergrowth of swamp vegetation, all but impregnable to human access. We turn to the right and see signs of civilization. Two or three cabins, little wharves washed by the ripples, a huge low-roofed sawmill, with its unceasing clatter and jets of escaping steam, and far in the distance, here and there, skiffs and wherries, each with their party of fishers, like ourselves, make up the scene, beautifully encased in a frame work of luxurious green. And the hushed peacefulness of the place, broken only by the whir of the saw-mill, the far-off shout of some successful angler, or the whistling of some swamp bird of brilliant plumage flying overhead, make us regret and almost forget that the noisy city and its daily toil are but two hours away.

Rowing on through these woodland shades, each dip of the oar recalls that sad story of Evangeline, who through such a scene wandered in search of Gabriel, her beloved. Longfellow's description of a Louisiana bayou is a perfect pen-picture. On yonder bank, it may have been that Gabriel was sleeping, while his loving and beloved Acadian maiden, after years of search, murmured, "something says in my heart that near me Gabriel wanders," and then passed sighing on, to years of gloomy repining.

But for such thoughts and memories as this, what care these two happy mokes, who seated in a small boat, with a lateen sail spread, come down the bayou before the wind, one of them at the helm, the other seated in the shade of the canvass, his chin deep in his left shoulder, and his right arm vigorously plying the bow across the strings of a rusty Cremona? Here is happiness for you. The artist is a spectacle by the way. A straw hat twenty years old, if a day, adorns his head, green goggles protect his eyes, and, as he answers a passing salute, in a basso-profundo which would drive Carl Formes to envy, there is a laughable lisp in his "How you wath to-day, thars?"

Now we are at the fishing ground, and we moor our boat at a landing consisting of a huge log extending into the tide. In the door of a cabin, newly built, not fifty feet off, stands a man in white shirt and trousers and straw hat. He is glad to see us, evidently, though this is our first meeting. "Anything further from the elections?" he asks, and having received in reply the morning papers, offers straightway the hospitalities of his ranche. He is evidently a character. His name is Murphy, and he has invented a hemp-breaking machine. He is a monomaniac, like all inventors—has his particular hobby, "hemp! hemp! hemp!" and has leveed in five hundred acres of this swamp for cultivation of his favorite product. It is curious to hear him spout Latin out here in these solitudes, and to hear him broach theories subversive of half the doctrines to which we have been brought up from childhood. He is a go-a-head American, though, every inch of him, and is living out here firmly believing that there is as much wealth for him in yonder swampy ground, as if he were to exhume some of Lafitte's buried gold.

But, Mr. Murphy, we came to fish, and can't listen all day to your philosophizing. The fish respond to our call; black-perch, sun-fish, crabs, snakes, shupecks, and all, come dangling through the air, and are landed on *terra firma*. This is certainly as splendid sport as we could have wished, and, this time, there is no Jonah in the party. The amusement soon becomes a labor, so successful are we, and keen appetite again reminds us that dinner time has come. Under a spreading tree we sit down, and conclude the repast begun in the morning. Then to fish again, while the elder Murphy emerges from his cabin, arrayed in gorgeous apparel, and, accompanied by the

A LOUISIANA BAYOU SCENE.

younger Murphy, a tall, well-built youth of twenty, jumps into a boat, hoists his sail, and saying, " Good day, gentlemen," is off for New Orleans.

And shortly after, we follow them, traversing the same watery path whose matinal beauties had charmed with their novelties and freshness. Our trusty Ethiopian, his mule exchanged for a rickety horse, awaits us at the designated point, and so, as the sun goes down in the west, we stand once more on the bank of the mighty river, and weary, yet pleased with the lessons of the day, begin again to think fondly of home scenes and associations in the great city slumbering yonder in the sunset.

"Why," asked F. O., pointing to a parrot, "is that bird like honesty?" and, without waiting for a reply, said: "Because it is the best poll I see."

QUERY.—If a man writes on parchment, is he necessarily on the ram-page?

A little darky, sucking molasses from a hogshead through a straw, is a vivid exemplification of the fact that the sweetest joys are those taken *syrup*-titiously.

THOMAS CAT IN TROUBLE.

Within the precincts of Philippa Street
Upon a housetop at the dead of night,
Careless of war's alarm, a Thomas Cat
Lay gently sleeping with extended paws,
And visage calm as if it ne'er had known
Those sanguinary conflicts, when the fur
Had flown, disastrously.
     Most plump was he,
And healthy, this grim prowler of the night.
For frequent forays on the larder he
Was famed, nor had the housewife's broomstick left
Unscarred his cuticle. That very day,
Detected whilst purloining, he had fled
And she pursued, aiming the while a brick
Which struck him on the caudal and evoked
A cry of mingled rage and agony,
As dashing o'er the cellar wall he cleared
The distance at a bound, and thence had sped
Him to the housetop, where beyond the reach
Of retribution, he devoured his prey
And fell asleep.
     But as he slumbered there
A roguish boy had spied his prostrate form,
From out a window that o'er-looked the roof,
And straightway formed a diabolic plan
To work his ruin. To this evil end
The youngster did procure a bit of cheese,
Affixed it to a hook of sharpest steel,
Attached thereto a fishing line and pole,
Then sent the dainty morsel dangling o'er

THOMAS CAT IN TROUBLE.

The nasal organ of the slumbering Tom,
Concealed himself the while yet peering out
Each little while to watch the sad result.

The mouser shuddering woke. Some game was near;
His optics opened wide—the cheese he saw,
He jumped, he bit, he screamed ow-yeouw-wiaow-wiaow—
Alas, within his ever hungry jaw
The treacherous hook had caught and now too late,
He sees the youngster, grinning with delight,
Proceed to pull him in. His plaintive cries
Resounded far and near, and from their lairs
Behind the chimneys and in courtyards dark
Came, summoned by unearthly cries of woe,
Tabbies and Toms unnumbered, all rejoiced
To witness in distress their common foe.
Meanwhile, the urchin tugging at his prize,
Had in the process managed to evoke
From Tom a series of such plaintive yells
That heaven and earth re-echoed with their sound.
And from the neighboring windows came a shower
Of bottles, brushes, missiles of all kinds,
Aimed by awakened sleepers at the head
Of Thomas. Thus it was, that as the boy
Convulsed with laughter paused to catch his breath,
He lost his hold, and lo, the mouser sped
With winged feet along the giddy height,
Dragging the pole behind him as he went ;
Nor paused until within the shade
Of steeple high and broad he drew his rein
And waited till the coming light of morn
Should bring to his assistance some true friend
To free him from his sad predicament.

THE STORY OF THE CHURCH TOWER.

I.

A sum of money had been stolen.

Such was the information given me early one morning by my very particular friend and crony, Joe Warren. He and I had been flogged together at school, had taken our first beer together in Freshman year at college, and graduating together, each with a better reputation for good-fellowship than for scholarship, had both of us settled down in the quiet seaport town of M—, where he had embarked in business as junior member of the forwarding and commission firm of Travis & Co., and I had leisurely devoted myself to Blackstone and Kent.

I was then occupying bachelor's rooms on High street. Joe lived at home with his mother and sisters, but visited me regularly. I was not therefore particularly surprised when, on the morning in question, he came rushing up stairs two steps at a time, and, without knocking, entered and shut the door with a slam behind him.

I was taking breakfast at the time. My matronly landlady but a few moments before had deposited on the table the waiter with its snow-white napkin, its hot coffee, rolls and boiled eggs, all scrupulously arranged in their customary corners. As Joe entered, I remember I held in each hand half an egg-shell reversed over the glass, into which the contents had fallen. His sudden entry did not cause me to desist from my occupation with any inordinate haste.

"Morning, Joe; draw up a chair," I said, looking up.

As I did so, I saw in his face an expression of unusual anxiety.

"Why, what's the matter?" I added.

"A sum of money has been stolen," he answered, looking at me in a sort of bewildered manner.

"Come, my good friend, keep cool," said I, "Sit down and tell me what is really the matter."

"Gone, sir, gone!—$3000 and over!" he replied.

I put down the egg shells, rose and walked to where he stood. "Joe," said I, putting my hands upon his two broad shoulders, "sit down."

Mechanically he sank into a chair; I drew up another facing him. "Are you cool?" said I. He nodded. "Then let's hear the whole story."

"Very well," he began; "but first strict secrecy I must enjoin. No one but myself knows what has happened. I went down to the office this morning, as I usually do on Mondays, a little earlier than usual; unlocked the door, went in, opened the shutters, and awaited the arrival of the boy who sweeps out the place every morning. It so happened he was a little late to-day.

I was walking up and down from corner to corner, whistling the moments away, when I suddenly spied upon the floor, near the sofa, what appeared to be part of a bank check. Stooping to pick it up, I found it was what I supposed. I took it to the window, where I could see more distinctly. 'sford' was all I could read upon it, written in a bold hand. Impatiently I sprang to the safe and picked up another fragment from the floor. Upon this I found a part of a stamp, with the letter W written on it by the cancellor. In a moment it flashed over me, "Weathersford." On Saturday evening, after banking hours, Allan Weathersford, who does business opposite, had given us his check for two hundred and fifty dollars or thereabouts, in payment of our interest in a consignment of merchandise, and this check I was certain I had deposited in the cash box and locked up inside the safe. To try the door of the latter was my next thought. It was fast; there was no sign of its having been touched since I locked it and put the keys in my pocket last Saturday evening. To unlock the iron door and peep in was the work of another moment. *The cash box was gone.*"

"You are perfectly certain of it?" I said inquiringly.

"Perfectly certain."

"And the keys of the safe have not been out of your possession since Saturday evening?"

"Not a moment."

"How much money was there in the box?"

"There was Weathersford's check, say $250. Two five hundred dollar bills that I was to have paid Captain A., who sails for New York at eight this morning. A package of fifty twenties. Three hundred dollars in gold that the mate of the Good Hope had deposited late Saturday afternoon, his vessel having just arrived from the Mediterranean; and then, let me see, some smaller amounts. I know I figured it all up on my way here. It must amount to at least three-thousand dollars."

I walked up and down the room two or three times, thinking the matter all over. "Joe," said I, ".can you get a duplicate check from Weathersford?"

"Possibly," said he.

"Do it, then. What time does Mr. Travis get down?"

"Never before ten o'clock."

"Good," I answered; "and Weathersford?"

"I never knew him to be later than seven, old as he is."

"Well, then, listen. We'll catch this sly thief; but everything depends on secrecy. How much ready money have you got outside of your business?

"Precious little," answered Joe, wonderingly. "Not over a thousand."

"Then I intend to lend you some."

"Nonsense, George. I won't have it."

"But hear me. I am willing to invest the amount of two thousand with Travis & Co. I have saved that much and more during the past three years."

"I won't hear of it."

"Not a word. You will when you find what I am up to. Now go you straightway to your office. Say not a word to a soul. Keep your safe locked. Leave your keys here, you'd better, so you can postpone opening the safe for an hour or two. Go over to old Weathersford. If necessary, let him into our plan; but at all events get the duplicate check. It is now half-past seven. Not a moment to lose, if you mean to pay Capt. A. those two five hundred dollar bills before he leaves."

Joe went down stairs in a hurry, as I had bidden him. I saw him around the corner, and was out myself. Three or four squares away I had occasionally noticed a money-broker's shop in passing. Thither I hurried. The boy was just taking down the shutters. "Is your master in?" I asked hurriedly? "At breakfast," he answered. "Well then, call him." In rushed the boy and out rushed the broker, napkin in hand. He was a florid faced, stout, elderly man, of short stature and smiling countenance. "Well sir," said he "what can I do for you so early this morning?" "How is gold?" I asked, hurriedly. "Thirty-five and three-eighths last evening," he answered. "Have you five hundred of it?" "Just that much," he answered, in a very business-like manner. "Do you wish to purchase?" "Yes, sir," answered I.

In ten minutes more I was laboring along with two heavy bags, one in each hand, towards the establishment of Travis & Co. In my pocket, too, were two five hundred dollar notes, which the broker had given me in exchange for smaller ones. As I turned the corner nearest my destination, a sea-faring looking man went brushing by up the street, grumbling something about "leaving keys at home, no way to do business." I laughed in my sleeve.

Joe was standing in the door. No one but the sweep had yet arrived. "The mate of the Good Hope has just been in," he said, "and grumbled like the deuce about that gold of his. I told him to come back in an hour and I'd have the safe open. He wanted to take the eight o'clock train."

"He can do it," I said, "Boy, run as fast as you can up street and tell that man with the pea jacket and fur hat to come back. The keys have come."

The boy was off like a flash.

"Now Joe, old fellow, here's the gold. Not a word— it's counted all right—saw it counted myself. Let the man have it when he comes."

Puffing and out of breath returned the boy and the pea jacket. "Came, did they?" said the latter.

"Yes," I said with a laugh, "here's the money."

"Not my money," he said, eyeing the bags.

"Five hundred in gold; I'll swear to it," said I.

"All right, gentlemen! Travis & Co.'s word's good for a thousand bags like these. Now I'll be off in a hurry to catch that train. Good morning."

"He's disposed of anyhow," said I; "How about Weathersford?"

"Hasn't got down yet. This morning, of all others, he's behind time. There he comes now, said Joe, and off he went to meet him.

A gentlemanly looking person with full beard, rather sunburned face, very well dressed, and with an agreeable manner, just then came in.

"Mr. Warren not here?" said he, pulling out his watch.

I pretended to be very busy. "Gone out, sir," I said. "Is there anything I can attend to for you?"

"Perhaps—yes," was the reply. I sail for New York at eight o'clock and wanted to get a draft on this house cashed before I leave, if possible; I can't understand how Mr. Warren can have forgotten this matter."

"Are you Capt. A. ?"

"I am, sir."

"He did not forget it," I said; "I have the money here to cash the draft; one thousand is the amount, I believe?"

"Yes."

"And you wanted it in two five hundred dollar notes?"

"Yes, if convenient?"

"There they are, captain."

He folded them up, put them in his vest pocket, looked at his watch again. "Jupiter!" said he. "I've but five minutes time ; tell Joe Warren I left my regards for him ; good bye t'ye."

Joe was just then coming out of Weathersford's ; he saw the Captain and called to him to stop.

"Good bye, Joe, old fellow," said the captain, as he ran; "havn't got time to stop; see you next trip."

And Joe, giving up the chase, came in, threw down the duplicate check, and said, "There we are."

"Did you tell Weathersford ?." I asked.

"No, he did'nt ask, only supposed we had lost it."

"Good! good!" said I; "now the gold is paid, Capt. A. is paid—here is the check—you have enough cash of your own to make good the balance, havn't you ?"

"About enough."

"Then," said I, "you'd better open the safe."

I know not which of us was the happier about that time. Joe and I had known each other too long and well to stop for any of those conventional words of thanks which would have been expected from the lips of a stranger. I confess, too, we were both of us a little bewildered with our heavy morning's work.

"Go ahead with business just as if nothing had happened, Joe ;" I said, "and come around to supper with me this evening."

"I'll come," he said, mechanically, with his head bent over the safe lock, inspecting it closely.

"I'll be there, George, at six o'clock."

"Why, Mr. Colton, you didn't half eat your breakfast this morning," said the cheery voice of my landlady, as I mounted to my lodgings again.

'No, I've been getting up an appetite though, Mrs. Snugley," I answered, closing the door.

II.

I lit my pipe, and taking a seat by the open window where I could view the street and the passers-by, fell to thinking of what I had done that morning. Now and then a momentary reflection stole over me, and whispered, " you're a fool to send your wits and your money wool gathering this way on the impulse of a single thought. Who would have done, or ever has done, as much for you? Now here this morning you have disbursed, nay perhaps thrown away, the neat little sum of sixteen hundred and ninety-one dollars and eighty-eight cents, with a very meager prospect of getting it back for some time to come, at least."

Now this thought I dismissed as often as it came. It only nerved my determination. "There has been a theft committed," I said, "*somebody* committed it. That *somebody* can be found, must be found, and now, having gone as far as I have in the matter, I am evidently the man to find him, or lose my money."

Just then I heard the clock strike nine in the neighboring bell tower. "Can't idle this way all day, Mr. George," said I, aloud, rising and taking a final survey of the street below. My eye fell on a cab that was driving rapidly up the street. Within it, was a pea-jacket, and within that, the same individual to whom the two bags of my gold that morning had been paid. He has missed the train, I thought to myself, and then I went to studying.

Joe came at the appointed time that evening, but looked very chopfallen and downcast.

"Why, you take on terribly about this affair," said I, after he had entered, and drawn up his chair to the table,

"Can't help it," he said, resting his elbows on the table, his chin on his hands, and looking at me, as if imploring me to help him unravel the mystery. "Everything went wrong to-day; Travis came down cross as a bear, because his pet Newfoundland was killed yesterday. There was a heavy fall in flour too, coming just after we ordered a large shipment. Look, I broke my watch guard, twirling it all day long with worriment."

"What killed the Newfoundland?"

"Poisoned, Travis says."

"Don't know who did it I suppose?"

"No; the servants say they saw a rough looking man hovering around the premises on Saturday night, and they set the dog on him. In the morning they found the poor brute lying dead on the door mat."

"Tell me, Joe," I said, "who keeps the keys to your office?"

"I do."

"And you took them with you after locking up on Saturday night?"

"Yes and had them until this morning."

"What kind of a lock is there on the safe?"

"Patent combination lock."

"No one, then, can open it unless he knows the combination of letters with which it was last closed?"

"Of course not; that's what makes the matter mysterious. I closed it on Saturday to the word 'Beware.' It opened to that same word this morning; and yet the cash box was gone."

"Very, very strange," thought I. "Do you never forget the word with which you have closed it?"

"I once did," answered Joe, "and had a locksmith that lives around the corner working for twenty-hours to get it open again. Since that I have kept a written list of words to be used on each day of the month."

"And that list is——?"

"In my pocket-book."

"Be perfectly sure of it."

He pulled out his pocket-book hurriedly. His cheeks turned ashen pale as he opened it. "Gone, by Jove," said he. "I had it last on Saturday evening. I remember getting out my pocket book, taking the word from the list, laying both book and paper down while I locked up. The mate came in just then with his gold, and I unlocked again on his account. I must have failed to replace the list in the pocket-book when I returned the latter to my pocket."

"And the mate—did he come out with you?"

"Yes. He appeared a little in liquor I thought. Every one else had gone, so I locked up and left him standing on the sidewalk before the store."

"Were there any marks by which you could identify the stolen bills?"

"None; but stay, I recollect one of the five hundred dollar bills was slit about an inch, and I pasted it together with a bit of tissue paper." For a few moments both of us looked up at the ceiling, uttering not a word. "Joe," I said finally, "you're tired out, you're miserable. Lie down on the sofa and take a nap. Make yourself perfectly easy in this matter. I think I've got our man picked out."

"He was yawning even then. "Well," he said, "I've let you manage this matter so far, and you may as well go on after your own fashion. When you need assistance call on me," and lying down, as I had bidden him, he was soon asleep.

Suspicion pointed unmistakeably toward the seafaring man, the mate of the Good Hope, I thought. The disappearance of the list of key-words, his presence in the office at the time, his willingness to accept the two new bags of gold that morning in place of the two he had deposited, and his not having taken the train after all, though in such apparent haste to take it, all looked unfavorable to him. But, then, the safe lock! Even knowing the key-word "Beware," how could this man have opened it? how could he, moreover, who had not been an hour in port, have prepared a false key to admit him to the building? Then again, the Newfoundland had been poisoned at Travis's house. Might it not have been a part, though a misdirected one of the same plot? Evidently, if this sailor committed the theft, he had a confederate, and one skilled in locks and keys. Now, would it not be well to see the locksmith, whom Joe had mentioned, and get his opinion, without, of course, giving him any clue to my object in asking it?

Acting upon the impulse, I put on my hat, left Joe sleeping soundly on the sofa, and hurrying down the street, soon found the locksmith's shop, a dingy, dirty little place, redolent with the odor of onions from the occupant's abode in the rear. The proprietor was in the shop, filing away by candle-light; nor did his features prepossess me, as, looking up from his work, he asked in a surly way, what I wanted.

"Do you mend safe-locks?" I asked.

"Sometimes," he answered curtly.

"What will it cost me to have a combination lock of six letters put in thorough order?"

He looked at me closely for a few minutes, and I, eager, apparently, for information as to the probable cost, looked him back. My glance seemed to reassure him. "About seven dollars," he answered, and looked down again at his work.

"And after it is once put in order you will guarantee that no one but yourself or those to whom you may explain the working, will be able to open it?"

"I'll guarantee that, yes." I thought the answer was a little surly again.

"Well, I may call again in the morning," said I turning to go.

The man called after me. "Perhaps you know Travis & Co. around the corner," said he.

"I don't know Mr. Travis," said I. "Why?"

"O, nothing, then; I mistook you for some one I thought I had seen there."

It was dark when I reached the street, but looking back into the shop through the dingy glass window, I saw a woman's face bending over the locksmith and looking inquiringly into his own. And at the neighboring gas lamp a man hurried by me; I could have sworn it was the wearer of the pea jacket. I stopped and watched him. *He entered the shop.*

"Joe," said I, shaking him, for when I got home he

was still sleeping, "Joe, I think that to-day we'll have them."

"Them?" he asked rubbing his eyes, "why, how many of them were there in it, pray?"

"Two, I think," said I, "for the present let me have it all to myself. You shall probably know it all to-morrow."

So he bade me good night then and there, and I myself, dismissing the subject for a while, very speedily thereafter bade the whole world the same.

III.

My morning paper was left quite regularly by the carrier, as indeed for two successive New Year days last past that peripatetic juvenile had most practically reminded me. Mrs. Snugley always brought it to my door betimes in the morning, and on rainy days even took the trouble of holding it before the kitchen fire to dry before throwing it in through the transom light. To read it before rising was an invariable and to me a delightful habit. And so it was that on the morning following the event recorded in the preceding chapter, even before my recollections of them dispersed by sleep had fairly returned, I found my attention attracted by the following paragraph:

"JACK ASHORE.—About ten o'clock last evening the denizens of the quiet neighborhood of Chippeway and Churchsteeple Streets were thrown into a state of unwonted excitement by loud cries of 'ship a hoy-oy-oy,' accompanied by a series of yellings, described as all but demoniac. The affrighted housewives, rushing to the doors or windows and peering out into the moonlight, were surprised at finding that the cries came from the vicinity of the church on the neighboring corner, and even appeared to proceed from the building itself. Two or three of the male residents of that vicinity hurried to the spot, and, upon coming nearer, found to their infinite amusement, an individual perched upon a ledge of the bell tower, only six or eight feet from the ground, clinging fast to an abutment with one hand, and with the other waving his hat and pea jacket as he cheered vociferously, 'Send us a boat won't ye?' A ladder was brought, and the drunken man, for such he was, having been, with no little difficulty, safely landed on *terra firma*, was conducted in a state of the utmost amiability and hilarious good humor, to the guard house, where he refused to give his name or occupation. His dress, conversation and general appearance indicate, however, unmistakably that he is one of those who go down to the sea in ships."

Can this be the mate, thought I. If so, what on earth was he doing in such a position? It had been about seven in the evening when I saw him dodge into the locksmith's shop. There were then three hours in which he might have managed to get himself sufficiently inebriated to attempt, at ten, the feat of scaling the belfry. But then, there were plenty of seafaring men beside himself in town. Yet, do they all wear pea-jackets? Mr. Mate, said I mentally, your conduct for the last twenty-four hours has been just a little suspicious. Now, should it prove that you are the individual referred to in this paragraph, those suspicions of you will be decidedly increased in my own mind.

I dressed and walked out, telling Mrs. Snugley that I would be back by nine o'clock to breakfast. It was a foggy, disagreeable morning, and I found the sidewalks slippery with mud as I picked my way toward the police station, which was half a mile away from my lodgings. The old station clerk was dozing in his arm chair when I entered, but the banging of the door made him jump to his feet, perhaps in anticipation of the arrival of another prisoner. He rubbed his eyes and said mechanically, "Good morning."

"Good morning to you, Mr. Clerk," I answered, "I see by the paper this morning that you have among your prisoners a sailor."

"And a right jolly one, too, sir," he answered, bursting into a merry laugh. "He wanted to treat the turnkey and me and all the prisoners and free lodgers to champagne last night."

I laughed too. "I called to ascertain," said I, "whether this good natured fellow is or is not a man with whom I am somewhat acquainted, and whose release, if it be he, I desire to procure."

"He's asleep, now, sir. I was in there five minutes ago, and saw him lying on the floor, with his coat for a pillow, and snoring away like one of the bulls of Basan.

But you can go in and see. Jim, let this gentleman look in at cell No. 3."

Jim rattled the key in the rusty lock, and I peeped through the grating within. There he was sure enough—the man to whom I had handed the two bags of gold, my gold; the man who had wanted to catch the train; the man whom I had seen in the cab, had seen enter the locksmith's, and now saw, with his unkempt hair over his forehead, sprawling on the prison floor. In another moment I was back in the station office. "That's my man, Mr. Clerk," I said, "how can I procure his release?"

"The magistrate's fine will be five dollars. Always is, in case of drunkenness. Leave that amount for payment when the case is called, and the prisoner can go."

"All right," I answered, handing him a five dollar note. "Now, I desire that you say nothing to this man concerning the matter of his release. Wake him up, and tell him he can go—that is, as soon as I have time to get out of the building," and suiting the action to the word, I thanked the clerk for his civility, and departed. Turning the neighboring corner, I stopped and waited. Presently the mate came out with his head hung down, and passing me, turned his steps toward the church, where the ludicrous scene reported had occurred on the previous night. I leisurely followed.

The tower formed the corner of the two streets, and was constructed of rough-hewn granite. There was an old tradition that the builder, being an irreligious scoffer, had at regular intervals in the structure on its front side, inserted stones fashioned as the ace of diamonds, clubs, spades and hearts, and pointing to them as the edifice rose, rudely called them the imprints of the devil's hand. Certain it was that the aces were there, and were invariably pointed out to visitors, with the additional statement that from the summit of that very tower on the day the church was completed the builder had fallen to the pavement below and met his death.

Before this tower the pea-jacket stopped, and here I stopped too, although I had noticed it a hundred times before, and, apparently unconscious of the other's presence, looked up mechanically at the ace of hearts which was nearest the base, and thence let my eyes wander to the ledges and pinnacles jutting out at intervals from the side. I observed that upon the four corners of each ledge (there were eight ledges as the tower tapered from the base to the summit) stood ornaments of stone, somewhat resembling an urn, or rather, perhaps a basin, and each set of them smaller than those on the ledge below. Those on the corners of the first ledge were, I judged, eight or ten inches in diameter, and about twice that in depth. As I looked, a white string, dangling over the edge of one of them, fluttered in the wind and caught my attention.

"Up early this morning, mister," said he, rather sourly

I thought. He was looking very dirty and sleepy. His eyes were bloodshot, his step unsteady, his glance nervous and uneasy; and yet he was perfectly sober, I could see.

"Why," said I, "you didn't catch the train, after all, eh?"

He started and appeared to remember the fact that he was to be supposed to have gone off on the previous morning. "No," he answered with an oath, "I am going to-day, though, or to-morrow at farthest; since I've had to stay, why a day more or less don't make much difference, you know."

"And have you any friends or acquaintances in town with whom you lodge meanwhile?"

"Not one," he answered.

"And where did you manage to find a comfortable bed last night?"

"At a lodging house down l y the water," was the reply.

"Umph," thought I, "he can lie without blinking. And," I added aloud, "you have risen early to take a morning view of the city under a fog, I suppose. By good chance your footsteps have brought you to its most interesting feature. In looking up you must have noticed the four stone aces inlaid in the tower wall."

"No," he said, nervously, lifting his eyes, as much to avoid mine, I thought, as to see what I pointed out. I told him the story of the builder. He grew fidgety and impatient with the recital. He wanted liquor I was well assured, but even an inordinate craving would hardly explain such uneasiness as he displayed, now looking up at the tower, now up and down the streets, and once in a while at me as I talked.

"And," I concluded, "a funny fellow tried last night, I see by this morning's paper, to invite just such a fate. Have you heard about it?"

"No," he said, with a look of surprise, "These newspapers seem to get hold of everything."

"It isn't to be expected any reporter would let such a laughable thing as this go by," I said. "Listen," and pulling out the paper from my pocket, I read the paragraph.

He laughed, but a sickly laugh it was, dying in the corner of his lips. "I must be going," he said in a husky voice. "This d—d foggy atmosphere sickens me."

"Well," said I, "good morning."

I had no idea, however, of letting him go far Before he had taken three steps, my foot was on a projection of the tower, and my hand grasped the damp mossy ledge above it.

"Why, what are you doing? You are not drunk, as the man last night was, are you?" he said, turning back, and even placing his hand on my leg, as if to dissuade me from ascending.

"Pshaw," I answered, looking down into his face, which now turned square and full toward me, and had a shadow of evil in its expression. "I'm a great climber, and to get up a little appetite for breakfast have determined to find out what that white cord that you see fluttering yonder is doing there."

"You shan't—you shan't," he said, almost in desperation. "Don't risk it. Let me go and bring it down for you."

"No, thank you," I said with assumed indifference, and lifting myself up to the ledge. "Here I am—safe, you see."

He begged that I would descend. I would not, but passing along to the corner of the ledge, took hold of the end of the tape and pulled. It was fast and did not yield to the strain. Another step, and I looked over into the urn or basin, over the edge of which it fluttered. *There were two bags marked "gold" lying there.*

"Somebody has taken a great deal of trouble here for nothing," I said, forcing a laugh and looking down at the mate who with a suddenly assumed braggadocio, asked "What is it?"

"Nothing here but some stones," I said, "and this cord tied around one of them."

The fellow turned pale, covered his face with his hands and cried like a child. "But let me look again," I exclaimed, "What, gold by Jove—why, here's a discovery." Down went his hands in an instant. "What," he said, "you say gold?"

"Two bags of it," I answered.

"Let's divide and say nothing of it," he said, with a low cunning in his look.

"Nothing of the kind," I said; "these bags must go to the police authorities to be advertised for a claimant."

Two mechanics, a young and a middle aged man, just then turned the corner on the way to their morning work. "Hullo," said the elder, "Mister, what are you doing up there?"

"I want you to witness," I said, "that I now hand you from this receptacle two bags of gold which I have found here and will deliver to the captain of police.

The men stared, as if they thought me crazy. "Gold!" they exclaimed.

"He's mad," interrupted the mate.

"Yes, gold," I answered; "here, catch this—careful now, there."

The young man caught the bag, I threw the second to his companion, and in another moment let myself down upon the sidewalk.

"Now," said I, addressing the workmen, "can you spare half an hour or so?"

The elder looked at the younger, they whispered together a moment or two, and the former said, "Mister, there's something wrong in this matter; if we can help to ferret it out, we're ready."

"Come along, then," I said, "and you, too, sir," addressing the mate, "suppose you join us."

"No I'm d—d if I do," he answered, looking doggedly at me and at the gold.

"Then," said I, "it will be necessary for me to compel you to go with us."

"Compel, is it?" he said with a devilish gleam in his eyes. "Come, young sir, we might as well settle it first as last, and right here. You've cornered me, curse you! and I'll have my revenge if I hang for it."

I could see the sheen of a knife blade in the air above me.

"Not so fast, my man," said the voice of my dear old friend Joe, and in another moment the mate lay sprawling on his back. It was all the work of an instant. The knife flew out of his hand. He struggled desperately, but Joe and I held him, and with the aid of an officer, attracted by the disturbance, reconducted him to the cell which he had left but an hour before. The two mechanics preceded us, bearing the gold, and, leaving their names and address with the authorities, departed on their way again.

"Joe," said I, "after we had got our prisoner safely under lock and key, "have you ever seen these bags of gold before?"

He looked at them, looked at me, half puzzled yet happy. "I put them in the safe on Saturday evening," he answered. "Here is the mate's name, as I myself printed it on each bag."

"Mr. Clerk," I said, "I wish to make a charge of attempted murder against the man just brought in."

He drew up an affidavit under my directions, and I signed it. "Now," I continued, "I want a search warrant issued. A heavy robbery of money has been committed. A portion of it is in those two bags. I have reason to believe that more is to be found in the premises to be searched."

Another half hour found Joe, myself and an officer entering the dingy shop of the locksmith. He looked up as we came in, and growled out a surly "What do you want?"

"Pardon us for troubling you, sir," I said, "so early this morning, but we have reason to believe that stolen money is secreted here. Mr. Officer, produce your search warrant."

The locksmith, evidently terrified, called out in a language which none of us understood, to some one in the back room. Quick as thought I sprang past him, and went in through the narrow doorway to a room which appeared to be devoted to the triple purposes of bed-room, dining room and kitchen.

The same face I had seen bending in the lamp-light over the locksmith's shoulder met mine. It was that of a young woman, neat in appearance, humble, even obsequious in manner. She approached me, and pointing to the bed whispered "There."

I lifted the mattress. There were the two bags of my own gold and there was a small cash box. I lifted the lid. There was money in it. "Joe," I called out, "come here." The officer remained in the shop with its proprietor. Have you ever seen this box before ?" I asked my friend. "*Mirabile dictu,* George," he answered, throwing up his hands, "you've triumphed."

I need not tell how the poor woman, an adopted child, or, perhaps rather, servant of the grim locksmith, told us all, and how in the narration she gloated in her revenge for long years of outrage; how the mate and her master had concocted the scheme during the Sunday previous, basing the project upon their possession of the list of key words to the safe; how on Sunday night they had gone out shortly after midnight, and returning an hour latter, brought with them the gold and the tin box; how the sailor had at once departed with the two bags of specie, to conceal them, he said, and had returned at daylight, laughing at the hiding place he had chosen; how, on Monday, he had deposited two other bags of gold for safe-keeping with the cash box; how he had returned that same night, quite tipsy, to quarrel with the locksmith, and finally, how since that time he had not returned at all.

That evening, I remember, there was a snug little dinner for three set at my rooms. Joe occupied one seat, I the second, and Travis the third. But it was not until we had reached our wine and cigars that the first managed to narrate to the third what had happened and what the second had achieved in their mutual behalf. "Gentlemen," said I, "do not thank me; "thank the reporter who wrote the paragraph 'Jack Ashore.'"

THE TRAGIC MEWS.—On Monday evening, while Jason and Creon were conducting an animated discussion upon the S—— Theatre stage, the audience was surprised by the apparition of a thomas-cat which, with crooked back, bristling hair, and elevated tail, dashed suddenly out at breakneck speed from behind the scenes, and crossing the stage, leaped off into the house and disappeared. Last night again the presence of pussy was perceptible, for from the upper gallery came, of a sudden, during the performance, feline cries of mingled hate and terror; cries which told of an approaching collision; cries succeeded by an intermingling of amorous squalls and caterwaulings; very funny perhaps, but nevertheless very annoying to those who desired to observe the performance closely.

SHAKSPEARE MODERNIZED.

A few days since a seedy loafer, who, despite his, blossomy and tattered garb, showed faint traces of better days, was arraigned upon a charge of having stolen a hundred dollars from a miserly old man. The circumstances of the theft and capture were too conclusive to admit of any denial on the part of the prisoner, who, to the surprise of all in the court room, put in a plea of "guilty" in the following words:

> Most sapient, shrewd and ever just recorder:
> Thou very knowing and astute official,
> That I have ta'en away this old man's greenbacks
> It is most true; true I have stolen them.
> The very head and front of my regret is
> There were no more. Light am I of touch,
> And skilled in taking all within my reach.
> For since these claws of mine had five years pith
> Till six months come September, they have used
> Their dearest action in the Workhouse shop.
> But little on that subject can I speak
> More than pertains to meats of broil and stew,
> And therefore little shall I help my cause
> By speaking of myself. Yet, by your leave,
> I will a round unvarnished tale deliver
> Of my whole course of crime; what thefts, what larcenies,
> What peculations, and what burglaries,
> (For such proceedings I am charged withal,)
> I won these greenbacks with.

The old man knew me; yes, he spotted me,
And seemed to wonder what I was about,
From day to day. The dodges, runs and hidings
That I have had.
I checked it through from when I first did see him.
Even to the very moment when I robbed him,
I knew 'twas courting most disastrous chances
Of moving off in yonder Black Maria,
Of hair cropped close, of prison coat and breeches,
Of being taken by the insolvent jailor
And put to labor. Yet, in spite of these,
To steal that cash I seriously inclined;
But still the old man hovered round the spot,
And ever as he'd turn his back to go,
He'd come again, and with a greedy look
Admire his treasured cash. Which I, observing,
Took once a pliant hour, and found good means
To snatch from him in haste the whole amount,
Which he in packages had hoarded up,
But not successfully. I then cleared out,
And round a neighboring corner disappeared,
Laughing the while at the successful stroke
Which I had made. His money being gone,
He gave me for my pains a world of search.
He swore it was a shame, a devilish shame;
'Twas pitiful, 'twas wondrous pitiful.
He wished he had not lost it, yet he wished
By heaven that he could do the same; he cursed me,
And bade policemen, if they did but love him,
To find the thief and bring his money back,
And he'd reward them. On this offer, I,
Grown daring by the dangers I had passed,
Went straight to him to claim the recompense;
And hence, your Honor, here you see me now.

THE IMP IN THE CLOCK.

One night as I slumbered, 'mid visions unnumbered,
'Mid fantasies wierd and forlorn,
While scenes ne'er enacted and dramas ne'er acted,
In wondrous succession were born;
While imps grim, unsightly, who visit me nightly,
Were hissing their oaths in my ear,
I heard a low knock, as if from the clock
That stood in the chimney-place near.

I heard it again: " 'tis naught but the rain
As it swiftly comes pattering down on the pane,
Or the pendulum ticking," I cried;
But the only reply, in return to my cry,
Was a knock in the clock at my side.

Though fearful and trembling, yet, courage dissembling,
I murmured in tremulous tone,
"Be thou angel or devil; good spirit or evil,
I order thee hence to be gone."

I shuddered with fear, for near to my ear,
In spite of the rain drops without, I could hear
A whisper as if from the dead.
Harsh, hideous, hoarse, cold, cruel and cross,
And telling of misery, woe and remorse,
In slow, measured accents, it said
"Come hither; unlock the door of this clock,
For here I'm a prisoner; what, do you dread
A poor little elf, of a size like myself,
Confined in this old oaken clock on the shelf?
I'd do you no ill, e'en had I the will,
And I promise your utmost desires to fulfill."

"Who are you?" I cried. "Old Nick," he replied.
"Some folks call me Satan; the Devil beside,
But come; set me free, I beseech you,
And treasures untold, both in jewels and gold,
I'll give you for ever to have and to hold;
Their marvelous uses I'll teach you."

"It sure were not wise, though great be the prize,
To set free in one's presence, the father of lies;
But it doth not appear, and I pray you make clear,
By what reason you chance to be prisoner here."

"Oh no! 'tis a secret that ne'er must be told;
But I'll give you a treasure more precious than gold:
If you'll liberate me you shall never grow old;
Your blood in its coursings shall never flow cold;
You shall wear the gift of immortal bloom,
Forgetful of misery, death and the gloom
Which e'er broodeth over the walls of the tomb."

"I know," replied I, "that ere long I must die;
The moments of lifetime are fast fleeting by,
Their limit each hour bringeth nearer.
E'en could I receive what you offer to give,
Do you think that forever on earth I would live
While in Heaven rest those who are dearer?"

"I know of a maid, young, comely and staid,
And radiant with beauty which never can fade;
With large, dreamy eyes of the tint of the skies,
When the moon from her starry couch seemeth to rise,
With lips of the rosiest hue;
And I swear by my head, be you living or dead,
No mortal beside you this maiden shall wed—
None other shall hold her than you."

"Ah! once did I love one as pure as the dove,
But now she is changed to an angel above;
Yet oft in the light of the still starry night,
I see hov'ring o'er me her cherub-like sprite,
And sad is her gaze as she chants the old lays
We once sang together in erst happy days."

"I have yet one treasure of worth beyond measure,
A fountain of endless, delirious pleasure,
A source of rare joy, unmixed with alloy,
Whose potency nothing save death can destroy.
It hushes all fears, it dries up all tears,
And the 'Water of Life' is the name that it bears
See! this shall be thine, this red, ruby wine,
Possessed of a potency pure and divine."

Then lo, and behold, a chalice of gold
Bestudded with jewels, of workmanship old,
Appeared in my hand and was raised to my lip.
Fore'er be accursed that long fatal sip.
'Twas luscious and tempting; still deeper I drank,
Yet no lower the wine in the gemmed chalice sank,
But it sparkled and glittered and wooed me to drink,
As I oft pressed my lips to its o'er brimming brink.

But hark! once again came that low single knock.
It recalled me to senses. I turned to unlock,
According to promise, the door of the clock.
But lo! it stood open—the goblin had gone,
Though not e'er his errand of evil was done,
For the cup is still mine, and the red ruby wine
Still within it doth endlessly, fatally shine.

BILOXI.

PROBABLY not one in a thousand ever heard of even the name of the quiet, dreamy village which, with a population of about two thousand, lies slumbering on the Gulf Coast, shaded by wide-spreading oak trees, and knowing no greater excitement the year round than the daily arrival of the steamboat from New Orleans. And yet, to our people, Biloxi is a word suggestive of summer recreation, of freedom from care and business, of a luxurious indifference regarding apparel, of salt-baths, snipe and Spanish mackerel, sail-boats and snoozes.

It is the oldest village on the coast. Here landed the Spanish adventurers and explorers, who, from Pensacola, wandered in their frail boats along the coast, searching for that great river, the discovery of which is thrillingly portrayed to every possessor of a five-dollar National bank-note. Here dwell to this day descendants of that valiant race, but, alas! most of them sadly degenerate, following the occupations of fishermen and boatmen, eking out a bare and scanty subsistence, devoid of any higher ambition than that of procuring their next day's dinner. Here, too, the French Creole element of Louisiana and its vicinity constitutes a numerous and a better portion of the population. You hear fully as much

Spanish (or Gascon) spoken as English, and as much French as both combined. There is an American streak in the community — a rising generation of tall, bold young men, who can aim a rifle or build and sail a boat as well as the best. There are churches, a public school, a Masonic hall, a market-place, one or two hotels, and any number of stores, where one may buy muslin or molasses, godly books, grindstones and gimlets.

As the first landing was made in this vicinity by the Spaniards, so it was by the Federal troops in 1861, and probably this was the only occasion when poor, tranquil Biloxi ever came to be generally mentioned in the Northern papers. I recollect that, early in the war, the New York *Tribune* published an editorial, the gist of which was, that the stars and stripes were at that time flying in every State then in secession. Mississippi was in that article represented by Biloxi, whither Butler had dispatched from Ship Island, about fifteen miles distant, a detachment of blue coats, who had landed and hoisted the United States flag over the court-house. The place was, however, only temporarily occupied, the New Orleans expedition necessitating the troops' withdrawal.

If you think it worth while, then, take a copy of Mitchell's or Colton's atlas, and learn with me the whereabouts of this quaint old place. Leave New Orleans at nine o'clock in the morning by the Pontchartrain Railroad, (the oldest in the country, and you would think so to travel over, it) and riding six miles through city and swamp, alight at the end of a long pier jutting out into Lake Pontchartrain, a little inland sea, the opposite shores of which are hidden by the horizon. From this point depart daily the Mobile steamers, and here, too, we find awaiting us the Laura, elegant, spacious and fast, built after the fashion of the Hudson River boats, her cabins carpeted, gilded, mirrored, a Steinway piano in the ladies' saloon, and marble pier tables for card players in the forward cabin. Really, no finer, better appointed boat could be found than this same Laura. We pay three dollars for our eighty miles sail and dinner in the prospective. Twenty-five miles, rapidly passed, bring us to the Rigolets, the deep, narrow sound or channel, bordered by meadow swamps, and connecting the lake with the gulf. Here, amid miasma and mosquitoes, which the colored troops manage still to fight nobly, stands Fort Pike, its barbette guns frowning sullenly down upon us as we whirl by. Further on, Pearl River, a silver thread winding through the green, empties its waters into the Rigolets, and far in the distance one may see, here and there, a snowy sail, rising as it were, out of the landscape. About this time the welcome sound of the dinner-bell summons every one down stairs to the after-cabin, where long tables flanked by white aproned mulattoes, spread their attractive contents before appetites sharpened by the salt air. There is the usual clatter, the usual confusion, the usual display of human nature in its best and worst phases, and then, lighting a cigar, we are up on deck again. The boat is now running along the open coast, distance two or three miles. On the right the sea, the boundless waste of water; on the left a line of unbroken pine forest, fringed with the whitest sand. Occasionally an island of an acre or two, an oasis of green grass, rises out of the water. This little group are called the Malheureuse Isles. Unhappy, indeed, must be he who even for an hour is exposed to their mosquitoes and mud. An hour more and the coast, hitherto running due east and west, trends northward, and the broad bay of St. Louis opens to the sea. Here it was that two or three little cotton-clads bravely came forth to meet the Federal gunboats in 1862. But the unwonted echoes of the cannon long since died away, and looking at the pretty town of Shieldsborough, or "the Bay," as it is commonly called, skirting the western shore, one can hardly believe that grim-visaged war has ever invaded this quiet spot. It is about three o'clock in the afternoon as we come alongside a wharf, from a quarter to half a mile long. The water is very shallow, and the pier head must reach the channel. Here are scores of people awaiting our arrival, wives and sisters, and daughters—summer watering place denizens—who consider it a sacred duty to be at the wharf-head daily when the boat arrives, whether they expect their husbands, brothers, and fathers or not. There are chattering darkies, country hoosiers, hotel agents, baggage carriers; in short, representatives of the whole population, all looking on, scrutinizing each arrival, or asking the news from town. So we leave them all and their pretty village behind. It boasts a weekly newspaper, a Convent, two good hotels, a Mayor and a Common Council, and has a population of about four thousand. Again we skirt the mainland, and six miles further reach Pass Christian, the most important town on the coast. Here reside in summer time many of the New Orleans nabobs, whose villas line the shore for a distance of six miles. There is a college here, a Masonic Hall, an Episcopal and a Catholic church, a steam mill, a market house and stores *ad libitum*. The resident population is much the same as that of Biloxi, whither we are voyaging. Ten miles further on a pier, nearly a mile in length, juts out into the Gulf, and we find ourselves at Mississippi City, a small place, yet important as the County seat. Here is the court-house, the jail, the clerk's office. Here at stated intervals, come quiet, long-headed, old-fashioned country judges to hold the sessions and decide between right and wrong. You may see on the walls in the court-room charcoal inscriptions made by the native soldiery in 1861. One, more ambitious than correct in his classics, has written: " *Qui sum cognosces ex* MEO *actionibus in futuro.*" Shades of Anthon, forgive him!

And now, we again turn our prow eastward, and just

as the sun is setting, behold the glimmer from the Biloxi light-house. Now the water is no longer shallow. We run close in to the shore, and the great waves from our paddles dash angrily under the village of bathing-houses, which, connected by little bridges with the land, stand at intervals of twenty feet along the water-front of the town. Before every place, too, there is a sail-boat at anchor, telling of a people fond of the sea.

At the landing may be seen a similar collection of expectants, the mail-carrier waiting for his bags, the white dresses and blue veils fluttering a welcome to dear ones, the Gascons jabbering away outlandishly about trifles. The boat goes on to Ocean Springs, the terminus, a few miles beyond, and now here we are at Biloxi.

The houses are small, mostly one story, the street, running along the water front, irregular in limits, and deep with white sand. Broad-spreading oaks are numerous, a board bench under each, and you may see many fences covered with seines hung out to dry. " Shady Grove House, sar—plenty fresh fish, fine clean bed, comfor'ble as you please," is the earnest address of an old darkey hotel runner. But we are not hotel goers. There is a neat rockaway awaiting us and our baggage, and in the space of two minutes by the watch we are riding along through the shady street toward the upper end of the village. Then come the piney woods beautiful in their evening stillness. Now we turn into a narrow lane, enter a gateway, and alighting in a court-yard darkened by the thick shade, are at our destination.

This old place is worthy of more than a passing description. It looks more like a Baronial chateau, or some old time country residence on the French sea-coast than an American homestead. It is only American in one sense at all events. Its owner and occupant, who lives here winter, and summer, is eighty years old, and commanded one of the companies that repulsed Packenham's troops at Chalmette on the 23d of December, 1814, and the memorable 8th of January, 1815. He is hale and hearty, and besides that, independent of all care, having made a fortune in the cotton business in New Orleans. He is a genuine Creole, of French and Spanish descent, and can give you the history of New Orleans and its people, from the days of palisades and stockades up to date. He is an epicure, and on his dinner-table can offer you a repast equal to any of Victor's or Delmonico's. He never drinks water; he says its is injurious to him. Claret is his mildest beverage, while upon his anciently carved sideboard you may have your choice of Absynthe, Maraschino, Curacoa, Sherry, Madeira or Alsopp. The plebeian whisky is a stranger here, but the absence is not felt. The house is a double two-story brick, facing the sea. You enter a broad gateway, and approach it by a bricked avenue, wide enough for the car of Juggernaut, with flower-beds and gras-plots on either side, and the never absent oaks, too. Step in upon the brick floor of this piazza, inclosed by a lattice reaching to the ceiling. Pass thence into a broad hall, running through the center of the house from front to rear. This is the dining-hall. The brick floor is brightly red, and clean as a frigate's quarter-deck. There is a broad hearth, suggestive of winter comfort, and the walls are hung with pictures provocative of an appetite. Doorways of oak, high and broad, open off into rooms on either side. We return to the piazza, and at one end see a winding stairway, leading to the front gallery above. We ascend, and enter the parlor, where a gloriously-toned piano, engravings of the First Napoleon's career, a well stocked library, and family portraits, nearly a century old, tell of cultivated tastes and their enjoyment. Off from the parlors the same oak doorways lead to bed-rooms as luxuriously furnished as the boudoir of a princess.

The grounds in the rear of the house are spacious. Yonder brick building is alloted to the kitchen and the servants. Further on half hidden by the tree-trunks, are the stables, the cattle-houses, the pigeon-house and fowl-yards. This little brick store-house, fitted up with shelves and drawers, is plentifully supplied with every kind of grocery, from *pates de fois gras* down to sacks of coffee and barrels of flour. Near the main residence is a long, low building, divided into five bed-rooms, which are kept always ready for the reception of guests. Throw open the doors, which perhaps, have not been open for a month before, and you find the room ready for your occupation, even to the smallest minutiæ of the toilet. There are libraries, lounges, and chess-boards here, all locked up awaiting the arrival of lucky guests. This is the bachelor's hall, or the *garconiere* as our host calls it, and here, wearied with our journey we fall to rest.

It is four in the morning when the old gentleman, three times the age of any one of us, raps at the door, and tells us that the fish are biting well this morning. We rub our eyes, and find it difficult to realize how this aged man can rise so early all the year round, ride to the village, spend his five dollars at market, and be home again before we younger city people are even stirring. Well, we fish in the gray morning from the end of the bath-house wharf, and, as the sun rises, return with a string of sheephead for breakfast. We welcome the family, whom we had not seen the night before; and sitting down in the portico of this old house built forty years ago, catch the cool morning breeze coming from the sea, and listen to the surf breaking on the other side of Deer Island, a long narrow sandy strip, covered with pines and palmettos, and running parallel to the coast, three-quarters of a mile away. Later in the day we jump into a row boat, and are on the island, which boasting two or three frame dwellings and a light-house, is yet melancholy in its solitude. On the beach in the fine white sand, you may see the tracks of snipe and heron. At that little cabin, midway from shore to shore, you may buy goats' milk at a picayune a glass, or may see in the distance a great black dog dashing through the shoal water, and actually catching and eating the small fish. This is about all there is interesting on Deer Island, and we float homeward again with wind and tide. There are fowling pieces in the dining-room, and all the other equipments of a sportsman. Go back in the woods and you may bring home a mess of *grassés* or *cailles*, or, on the beach, and a lot of snipe, or, perchance, a Mallard duck, awaits your aim. Then there is a sail boat at your disposal, provided you are not timid of the squalls and thunder-storms which sweep these waters so suddenly and so often.

In short, this is the spot where real enjoyment, real hospitality may be found. Think of eating for dessert a pineapple picked in the hot-house only an hour before, and flavored with the choicest white wine; or of smacking your lips over sherry older than the house itself, and all this luxury in the country, far away from New Orleans; in fact, right in the piney woods. And then, when night comes, you may sit and smoke in the moonlight on the front piazza, looking out on the sea, and listen to the old traditions of the pirates who landed here, and of even the red men before them, until the figure of Lafitte seems to loom up on the beach before you, and you find yourself falling into a nap.

THE MAPLE LEAF.

A withered leaf fell from a maple tree
   That swaying, bowed beneath the autumn wind,
Rustling the while its mournful memory
   Of summer's verdant glories left behind.

On mother earth's fair bosom, damp with dew
   Of earliest morn, the leaflet, flutt'ring fell,
Then, bounding off upon the breezes, flew
   Forever from the spot it loved so well.

And, as through dell and woodland shade 'twas borne,
   O'er meadows green where murmuring streamlets flow,
But one sad plaint went with it, all forlorn
   As with a shell, its seaside echoes go.

Till, falling where a river, swift and wide
   Flowed on in silent grandeur to the sea,
'Twas borne along upon the eddying tide
   Mid sunlit ripples dancing merrily.

Forgotten then the still secluded glen
   Where grew the maple tree that gave it birth;
Forgotten all its plaintiff murmurs then;
   Forgotten all save joyful gleeful mirth.

Ah! ye who from the home of childhood stray
   To wander o'er the stranger scenes of earth,
Let not that first loved vision fade away.
   Forget not thus, in exile, all its worth.

THE BLISS OF BOARDING.

The everlasting bell rings you up in the morning, provided you have been able to sleep through the racket created beforehand by noisy domestics (unbleached) who rush hither and thither, indulging in occasional refrains from Delahanty and Hengler, and illustrating the same by some scientific movements on the heel and toe in the hall. The boot-black officiates also as bell-ringer, and as he goes his rounds from door to door, with brush and box, lugs the bell with him, its random taps effectually barring sleep, and giving a foretaste of what is to come when the boot-black shall cast aside his menial implements and rise to the dignity of a bell-ringer.

If the chambermaid, who, being comely, is, of course, worthless, has deigned to leave towels and fill your pitcher last evening, you may, as soon as the ding-dong has died away, rise and perform your ablutions. If, on the other hand, the delinquent fair has devoted too much of her time to coquetting with a gallant fair-laddie across the way, and has thus left your washstand forgotten, you must go unwashed; for to raise the window and shriek at the top of your voice for a servant were worse than useless, even though a dozen of them hear you calling. And even should one of them inadvertently pass your window, and receive your instructions, he goes off promising to comply, yet that's the last of him. And what's the use complaining to the landlady? Bless her, weak-minded woman as she is, do you suppose she has the slightest control over these strapping negro boys, who, by the way turn out in every Radical procession, and groan her when they march by the house? No, indeed! Why only a few days ago they mutinied in a body, upon the occasion of the employment of a great black fellow as steward to oversee them, and presented their ultimatum; they would leave, or the new nigger must. Well, they had been there a good while, you know, and knew which of the boarders would put up with small pieces of beef or a cup of stale coffee; moreover, they waited for their wages longer than most servants would, so the old lady concluded to surrender at discretion, and the mutineers returned to duty.

Well, you finally manage to reach the breakfast table, after serious misgivings that your fine tooth-comb has left one or two teeth in some kinky head during absence yesterday, and a gnawing suspicion that your tooth-brush has been similarly tampered with. But, in the solemnity of the ceremonies attendant upon the interment of breakfast, you relapse into a dreamy forgetfulness of the outer world, and its trivial annoyances. By most of your fellow-mourners a proper decorum, a touching appreciation of the sad occasion is evinced. Few are there sacriligious enough to break the impressive silence by raising their voices above a whisper. One gentle weeper mildly whispers to her spouse that, " hash never did agree with her," and then timidly glances at her *vis-a-vis*, the Captain, a ferocious fellow with a mustache, who, whatever may have been his exploits in the tented field, here displays a lamb-like submissiveness. Down near the far end sits an individual bearded like a pard, seedy in appearance yet desperate in demeanor. He alone dares break the silence, and the serious family start with horror as he ejaculates: " Take away that d—d beef-steak and bring me something to eat." The landlady confidentially informs you that this individual owes her for three months' board, and she does wish she could get it; that furthermore he is out late every night, and invariably comes home tipsy, and worst of all, that he is suspected of Radicalism and has never publised a card denying it.

What a horrible man! And yet he don't seem to care, as he scatters devastation around him. Whole plates of biscuits disappear as quickly as under the magic wand of a Haselmayer, and enormous quantities of baked potatoes, hominy and coffee go down his throat in rapid succession, while his victim hostess indignantly watches his exploits from afar off.

All boarding house inmates are classified into two kinds,

the good paying genus and the delinquent genus. And yet, to belong to the former class does not always imply that your character will be safe from scandal, or that your reputation will pass unscathed through the gauntlet of jealousies or downright malice and slander in which your delightful companions or your landlady indulge. They will visit your room, borrow your things, chat with you confidentially about this one or that one, and presto—change—go off to report. The room of the *passe* widow, located somewhere off in the recess to the rear of the building, is the headquarters where all discoveries are regularly reported and recorded, and whence, in turn, they are retailed in small lots to suit the curious. Here, at early dawn and eve, the gossips assemble. Here come the nurses bearing the family secrets of their employers; here, too, the children, who, being duly quizzed and cross-questioned, in their innocence afford valuable disclosures regarding the price of mamma's new bonnet, or how late papa came home last night. The information once obtained is borne upon the wings of speed to the other inmates, and thus every one manages to keep tolerably posted in regard to every one else in the house.

And perchance some day you come home feeling tired out, resolutely resolved upon an afternoon snooze at all hazards. Ah! charming discovery! the plasterers have taken possession, and, in compliance with directions from

THE BLISS OF BOARDING. 133

a beneficent and obliging landlord, are going to make the house "as good as new" inside and out. If you never swore before, you certainly will upon finding your only suit of black clothes, which you left hanging upon the door, thrown indiscriminately together under the mosquito-bar, and even then somewhat spotted with whitening; your toilet table moved out into the hall, your brushes, combs, mirror and other paraphernalia hustled away somewhere; your wash basin half full of lime, and your floor so bespattered that even to cross it is disagreeable. Two ladders have been hoisted, and upon the top of each, whistling and in a happy indifference of having invaded your domestic sanctum, and dashed down your Lares and Penates, stands a paper-capped workman, who glances down at you as much as to say, "What do you want here?"

Passing through L—— Square, yesterday, one might have seen a happy old negro, seated upon the border of one of the grass plots, his back against a tree, his face upturned, his mouth wide open, his eyes tight closed, asleep. By his side rested a saw, a buck and all the other lesser implements of the wood-sawyer's avocation, and above his venerable head, from off which the hat had fallen, hovered swarms of tantalizing flies and mosquitoes occasionally lighting on his nose, yet failing to disturb his slumbers.

A LOCAL SKETCH IN VERSE.

It was upon St. C—— Street,
There stood a hungry wight,
A seedy coat upon his back ;
'Twas twelve o'clock at night,
The last street car was rattling past,
The rain was falling cold and fast.

He stood before a window,
'Twas filled with viands rare ;
Poor devil !—how he longed to taste
Those dishes resting there ;
For, save upon a crust of bread—
That day the fellow had not fed.

Roast beef was there in plenty,
And flanked by fruits and fish,
Were huge boiled hams and turkies fat,
And many a tempting dish
Collected from the earth or sea
To tempt poor devils such as he

Now, as he looked with longing
Upon this varied store—
" Thou art so near and yet so far,"
He murmured o'er and o'er,
Fixing the while his gaze intent,
Yet knowing that he'd not a cent.

Within was heard the clatter
Of fork and spoon and plate,
As waiters bustled here and there,
And men their victuals ate,
They had no earthly thought about
The fellow cold and wet without.

He gazed another moment,
Once more he glanced within—
Then struck his empty pockets
And eyed his trousers thin;
He felt as Cæsar must have done
When plunging in the Rubicon.

Then with an air of boldness
He opened wide the door,
And, with the mien of millionaire
Strode o'er the sanded floor.
Then, at the counter, very cool,
Sat down upon a velvet stool.

"Bring me a cup of coffee,
 With milk," he boldly cried—
"And let me have a slice of duck,
 I much prefer outside;
And then, too, waiter, you can bring,
Some bread, potatoes—anything."

And as the waiter started,
Again he called him back—
"I'd quite forgot; a turnip, with
That slice of canvass back,
And if you've any venison fat
I don't mind having some of that.

"And oh! see here, please, waiter,
  Before you further go—
Be sure that those potatoes
  Are nicely browned, you know."
The waiter nodded, but a glance
Upon the stranger cast, askance.

But very little cared he,
  Though hungry, tired and wet,
For all the waiter's glances,
  He eat, and eat, and eat,
Until around him lay a heap
Of empty dishes two rows deep.

"Now bring me an Havana,"
  He said in blandest tone,
"A toothpick, too," he added,
  The waiter gave a groan,
His seedy guest remained so long
He half suspected something wrong.

"Now, waiter, what's the damage?"
  "Three dollars and a half."
"Why bless me, that's a trifle,"
  He answered with a laugh,
"Or would be had I funds—I meant,
But, my good sir, I've not a cent."

"What! do you mean to tell me
  That all you've eaten here
Shall not be paid for, mister?"
  "That is the case, I fear,"
Replied the other—"I must say,
I hav'nt got a sous marque."

A LOCAL SKETCH IN VERSE.

Then in a towering passion
Th' indignant waiter ran
Upon the street and straightway called
A Metropolitan,
Who led him to the calaboose
This diner upon duck and goose.

And there incarcerated
Within a dingy cell,
He lay and slept full satisfied
That he had dined so well.
And so mid shouts and drunken screams
Let's leave him to his prandial dreams.

"Go in, and put on one of them armors," was the peremptory mandate we heard given in passing the stage entrance to one of our theaters last evening. Don't you know what an armors is?" The question was addressed by an inferior attaché in his shirt-sleeves, to some ambitious youth whom he had recruited to serve as a warrior in the mimic battles of the evening. "No, what's armors anyhow," inquired the newly enlisted, evincing aught but that military respect for superiors, which is supposed to control the mail clad henchman. We didn't stop to listen further, but the training of that chap in rehearsal must have been rich.

ON THE RIVER.

An afternoon ramble on the levee, a quiet contemplation of the shipping, the boats, the city, the mighty stream silently rolling by, are not the least among the enjoyments which may be crowded into a leisure hour or two. And so it happened that on Sunday, as the sun began to go down into the west, we found ourselves strolling along the wharves, our attention about equally divided between the sights afloat and ashore. Now a little tug would go puffing by, making more commotion with her pipes and paddles than one ordinarily hears from an ocean steamer. On the other hand, a score or two of children, decked in holiday dress, came romping, laughing, past, closely followed by as many nurses, who had evidently taken advantage of "Susan's Sunday out" to hold council over their common domestic grievances. Yonder lies, moored to the bulkhead, a great black hulk, silent and motionless, which but a week ago was buffeting the waves of the Atlantic, and here, on our left, comes scudding down before the wind a feminine craft, rigged out in gaudy colors, evidently bent on conquest. The cool evening breeze is blowing, and the atmosphere is clear and bracing.

We lean over the bulkhead, and watching abstractedly the muddy current, eddying past, fall to thinking. Our thoughts run up stream, though, and retrace these waters to their source, far up among the Western hills, where, bubbling from the earth, a thousands springs supply as many rivulets of cool, crystal water, pure as the life of man in infancy, and yet, like it, destined to mingle with baser elements. But it will mix with the waters of ocean and there be cleansed of its impurities; it will flow through the dark caves where the coral insect is at work; it will perchance lave the shores where the sands are golden, and where palm trees rise, or will float upon its bosom some towering iceberg, straying—

"All aboard for Carrollton" were the words which, uttered in a business-like voice, banished our musings and wound up the soliloquy. Looking up, we saw a boat, a large boat, her bow at the landing, a throng upon her deck, volumes of black smoke issuing from her pipes, and giving indications of immediate departure. There was but a moment to lose, but in that moment we jumped aboard, and found ourselves booked for Carrollton on the A. G. Brown.

To find a comfortable seat on the hurricane deck, and to light a cigar, were the next steps to be taken, and then came the real comfort of the trip. There is but little opportunity to observe the numbers around us, who, like ourselves, have wandered for awhile from the city. There is enough to do in watching the thousand-and-one objects that present themselves along the route. Here a party of adventurous boys, shouting and laughing, pass almost under our paddles, their skiff lifted like an egg-shell on the waves in our wake. Yonder, lies moored a flat-boat, just such as we have seen in that engraving of "The Jolly Flatboatman." Now we pass the stock landing, and, looking up the broad green avenue, running back to the interior, can see it dotted here and there with horse-cars. There is a grain elevator below there, and above, standing out in relief against the leafy background, are the Louisiana Ice Works; opposite, the twin towers of the Harvey House may be discovered, a landmark familiar to fishing excursionists. The cool breeze of evening is blowing, and looking back at the city growing smaller in the distance, we inwardly thank our stars that we jumped aboard, and for awhile have bid adieu to *terra firma*. All along yonder bank, people are out enjoying the holiday, and appear to cast rather envious glances upon us as we pass. Here are moored whole acres of rafts, made of immense logs floated from the far-off forests of the upper tributaries; further on, a fleet of barges, laden to their fill with coal, destined at some time or another to pass up in smoke through the chimneys of this great city. And now we see the broad level meadows of Greenville, with here and there a clump of oaks, beneath the shade of which reposes some quiet home. Here, near the margin, embowered in a beautiful grove, stands the Sedgwick Hospital, and, on the little wharf before it, a knot of soldiers are gathered, smoking their pipes, and evidently hoping that there is no more fighting to be done. Below, on the boiler deck, a gang of lusty Africans are chattering away over their pot of steaming coffee, the fragrant fumes of which come to us with no unpleasant reminders of bivouacs and early breakfasts. Now we are opposite Carrollton; again the streets and squares assume a tangible shape, and in the distance the roof of the Court house and the spires of the churches may be seen. In a moment more, a dull thump and a stoppage of motion tell us that the boat has landed, and then, mingling with the throng and bidding adieu to reverie, we find ourselves once more ashore. There is a horse car just starting from the depot on the other side of the street. It is filled with people who have been rambling through the beautiful walks of the Carrollton gardens. But never mind; there is always room for more, so we jump in and in half an hour are back again in the city, fully convinced that at least one Sunday afternoon has been pleasantly and profitably spent.

THE REQUITAL.

CANTO I.—THE SAD CHRISTMAS.

'Twas in the twilight of a Christmas Eve
That two fond hearts were parted. They had loved
Each other long—if long, indeed, were years
Through which young love grew stronger day by day,
Making the months pass e'er more fleetly by.
And yet within those hearts, through all these years
There had been, oft, misgivings; vague, 'tis true,
Flitting athwart the sunlight of their lives,
As on a showery day in balmy spring
Dark shadows flit across a landscape green,
And tinging o'er the hues of happy hours
With a dim vapor of uncertainty;
E'en creeping in between each lover's kiss
To steal away its sweetness from them both.
But when, as oft, in puzzled mood they'd ask,
"What is there that is lacking in our love?"
The undefined answer never came,
And so they left the question in despair,
Till their own hearts should ask it them again,
  His was a heart that ever knew unrest.
From early boyhood, nothing had he known
Save longing for some better thing beyond
That which the present brought. In vain he strove
To drown his restlessness in study, and
Vainly had Pleasure wooed him to forget,

The ever present yearning for that Peace
Which to unquiet natures such as his
This world, alas! can never, never give.
  But when, admired and courted by the world,
Proud in her beauty, peerless as a queen,
Yet with a calm sweet face that told of pure,
Untarnished soul within, she came before
His vision, 'twas to whisper to his heart,
"Here is the rest which thou so long hast sought,
Here the fulfillment of thy life-long dreams."
Then, from that hour his very life was changed,
Forsaken were his books, his revels then,
A single purpose settled in his mind;
To win the heart, the life, the love of her
Who thus unconsciously had promised Peace.

It came. For on a starlit night in June
While fireflies glimmered 'midst the leafy shade,
Where they alone were seated, did he tell
The story of his life, his hopes, his doubts,
And forth from the recesses of his heart
Came bubbling up, as clear as crystal drops
The new resolves.
  Then with uplifted eyes,
"Ah, Gerald," she had said, "I little thought
That pity for your soul's unhappiness
Would thus have grown to earnest, fondest love:
At first 'twas but compassion that I knew,
Yet, watching day by day your valiant strife,
On my behalf to overcome yourself
And be what you did think I'd have you be,
I've longed to join in battle by your side:
Compassion into purest love has changed;
Henceforth, my life, my love are only yours."

THE REQUITAL.

    Thus, as two children on a sunny day
Meeting, 'midst flowers, join hands and wander on
Together, weaving garlands as they go,
To decorate their brief acquaintanceship,
These two did wander through the summer hours.
Each day, succeeding day, brought with it naught
Save fresher wreathes with which to crown their hope.
But oft concealed among the roses, thorns,
So closely interwoven that in vain
They sought to pluck them out, would madden Hope
And tempt her to foreswear their votive boons.
Ah! vague unrest—again he felt its power.
At times he said she did not love him well,
And she in tears would tell her love again—
But, oft repeated, this a habit grew
Until she had mistrust of her own heart,
Fearing her love unable to withstand
These most unjust suspicions.
                Thus it was
That in the twilight of a Christmas Eve,
The third that followed their bethrothal, she,
Through eyes all tearful looked a sad "Good Night."
And bade him gentler be when next they met;
While he, repenting of the cruel words
To which exacting love had prompted him,
Promised that with the morrow's festal dawn
Should come a brighter sunrise o'er their hearts.
    That morrow's sunrise never came for them;
That Christmas day was drear and desolate;
For to him, strengthening the stern resolve
To conquer his mistrust, a missive came,
'Twas heavy with the ring he'd given her,
'Twas written in her own familiar hand.
" No longer," wrote she, " can my heart endure

These oft-recurring trials of its love ;
'Twere better that we never meet again
Than that the painful scene of yesterday
Be re-enacted. May the God above
Who knows our griefs, have pity on us both.
Gerald, farewell."
    That morning he had sought
And found a snow white lily which within
The hothouse warmth to fullest bloom had grown,
And this, that day he would have given her,
An emblem of their happy days to come.
But now—he crushed its petals in his grasp
And, angry, ground them 'neath his foot, until
Their fragrance rising told him all was o'er.
He bowed his head and murmured, "But a dream."

CANTO II.—THE LONG YEARS.

Now all his passions long restrained, burst forth ;
The Evil in him, which, but yesterday,
He could have trampled down—nay, which he thought
He had completely conquered, now rose up
With giant strength, enthralled no more, and said,
. I am thy master, for no longer now
The Good contests my sway."
      'Twas bitterly
He did acknowledge this and yielded ; then
Away was straightway hurried to a life
Of sin so dark that not a ray of good
Its gloom could e'er illumine. Oft in vain
Her image prayed him pause. Yet with it came
Not Hope, so nothing recked he of the prayer.
Then for long months upon the weary bed

Of pain he tossed, and o'er him hovered shades
From Death's dark shore, yet still he thought of naught
Save that great disappointment. Then, one day,
As with returning life came new desires,
And the determination that that life
Should be a triumph over self, there came
Another blow, more cruel than before.
That heart and life which she had promised him,
And him alone forever, were bestowed
Upon another. But a year had passed,
Yet had the wounds of separation healed,
And she, with an unpitying hand, fore'er,
Had closed the gates of possibility.
  That moment cast its shadow o'er his life.
He blamed her not; perhaps 'twas generous.
Yet when the fiery storm of woe had passed,
He could not find it in his heart to think
Of her with aught save that same ardent love
Which on the quiet starlit night in June
He once had proffered her.
                     Then far away
To other scenes his fortunes carried him;
Yet with him went the ever present thought
Of her. Then by degrees, with time there came
Indifference. He wearied of the round
Of dissipation and bethought himself
T'were folly thus like prodigal, to waste
The energies which God had given him.
To waste them, and for what? The loss of her
Who knowing his dependence yet had cast
Him from her cruelly? Nor only this—
He still had health, had mind, had his right arm
Wherewith to cleave a pathway to success.
Why then should this pale shadow intervene,

More potent than a score of steel-clad foes?
"Delusive grief, thou shall not haunt me more;
Make way nor longer cumber up my path,"
He cried, and brandishing the sword of Will,
Beat down the specter, and once more—was free.
   And meanwhile what of her? She deeply felt
The pain he suffered. She had known too well
His ardent nature, not to be assured
That separation brought a train of woes
Unspeakable. Yet, on her bended knees
She prayed for counsel, and in tears beheld
The path of duty plainly pointed out.
Once more compassion took the place of love.
She watched his course of life yet stood aloof,
Full sure that but a word of pity would
But uselessly revive his quenched desire.
She found she had not loved him, and recoiled
From contemplation of the misery
Which might have followed the discovery
Too late of her mistake. It was regret,
And not remorse that she experienced
In thinking o'er the grief which she had wrought.
Society, pretending sympathy,
Once more environed her with flatteries,
And wooed her once again to its delights.
With aching heart she followed the behest,
Yet looked with coldness on her flatterers,
And longed the while for thoughtful solitude.
   One day there came a missive. It was signed
With Gerald's name. 'Twas he had written it,
Returning from a night of revelry;
And these the words that he addressed to her:
      "Ah, why did I ever dare doubt you?
      Forever I'm grieving about you;

I cannot be happy without you.
Come back to me, darling, I pray;
Come back to me, dearest,
Oh, why should the merest
Coventional trifle
Thus endlessly stifle
The love which I know
Is lurking below
In the innermost part
Of your once tender heart?"
Hot tears bedewed the paper as she read,
"Oh Gerald, Gerald," sadly murmured she,
"God be the judge between us."
    Then with time
And the solicitations of the world
She yielded up her hand, perchance her heart,
To one who gave her home and happiness.
Domestic cares and duties dulled the edge
Of memory, yet once she told to him,
The partner of her life, the history
Of that mistaken love, and he in turn,
With tenderness had bade her dry her tears
And think of it no more.
    His bidding was
Her law, his wish her own; and thus it was
That faded fast thenceforth from out her soul
The vision of that starlit night in June,
And of that tearful twilight Christmas Eve,
The Alpha and Omega of a love.
In course of time, about her children played;
And often looking in their faces fair,
With all a mother's tenderness, she'd pray
Their future lives had not in store for them
A trial such as that which she had passed.

CANTO III.—THE MERRY CHRISTMAS.

And Gerald, too, in that far distant clime,
Subduing, not forgeting his regret,
Had found a fond companion of his life,
And happy in a wife's and children's love
Was plodding on, a sober, earnest man.
Through all these years not once had he beheld
The dear old home where childhood's scenes were laid,
And oft a longing heartfelt, aye intense,
Stole o'er him to revisit that loved spot
And bringing with him to his parents' side
The rosy featured idols of his heart,
Say—"See the treasures God has given me."
And with the thought, there came another. 'Twas
The wish that she who once had cast him off
Perchance in misery and gloom to die,
Might know his triumph.
    And within his heart
This constant fixed assurance ever dwelt,
That surely as the sun did shine in Heaven,
Their tearful parting on that Christmas Eve
Was not their last. That they would meet again,
And make their peace, he was as certain as
He was that she had once possessed his love.
Seas might divide, or death might threaten them—
'Twas naught. They yet sometime should meet again.

And thus it came that on an April day,
And at the hour of sunset, Gerald stood
With folded arms and thoughtful brow, erect
Upon a vessel entering the bay,
Whose waters laved the spot where he was born.
With beating heart he saw once more the home

Wherein his childhood passed, the trees, the spires,
And all the thousand objects long forgot,
Yet now familiar to his memory.
A tear unbidden trickled down his cheek,
As of his heart he asked inquiringly,
Why he had ever left a scene so dear ;
Then all at once he spied a snowy sail,
And then another—and another, still,
Go flitting by athwart the vessels prow,
A little tiny fleet of pleasure boats,
Each laden with its freight of joyous souls,
While ever and anon across the tide,
Glassy and placid 'neath the setting sun
Was heard the grateful harmony of song
Or childish laughter borne upon the air.
    But e'en as Gerald gazed, a piercing scream,
A wail of agony unspeakable
Came mingled with the mirth and melody.
" Great God, have mercy," 'twas a mother's prayer,
She sees her darling, fair-haired, first-born child
With arms outstretched for succor, disappear
Beneath the wave ; all this, too, Gerald saw,
" God give me strength," he murmured inwardly,
" By this redeeming action to efface
The Evil of the Past." Then, quick as thought
Sprang bravely over the taffrail ; 'neath the wave
An instant disappeared, then rising, pressed
With sturdy strokes toward the very spot
Where last the golden ringlets of the child
Had vanished.
            Look ! again the little hands
Arise to pray for rescue, and again
Go down. Ah, God—'tis vain, too late, too late !
Now, Gerald give fresh impulse to thine arm,

A second now were worth a score of years.
There—there—he's reached the spot, and disappears
Again, but quickly rises—God be praised,
The child is saved. Its dripping ringlets fall
Upon his shoulder, and its pallid face
Upturned toward the setting sun, doth yet
Give hope of life within. A moment more,
And weary, yet triumphant, Gerald stood
Upon the sailboat's narrow deck, his arms
Outstretched to give the mother back her own.
He lifted up his eyes and, in the glance,
Encountered hers—those same, sad, thoughtful eyes
Which on that ne'er forgotten Christmas Eve
Long years before - (it seemed but yesterday,)
Had bid him be more kind when next they met.
She did not shun the glance. She only knew
That he, as one who cometh from the dead,
Had come to save her well-beloved one.
"Oh, bless you! bless you, Gerald! God will give
His recompense for this good deed of yours,"
She said, and clasped the now reviving child
To her fond mother's heart.
      Her words to him
Were full repayment for the weary days
Of anguish and regret. He kissed the child,
(His heart was then o'er full for utterance,)
And bowed his head in grateful reveries.

Another scene and all the tale is told,
A score of years have come and lived, and gone
'Tis Christmas Eve again, and merrily
The vesper chimes come tinkling on the air
From out the belfry, joyous messengers
Of peace and God's good will to all on earth.

They found an echo in two happy hearts,
A manly bridegroom and a maiden fair.
Who kneeling at the chancel steps before
The altar, heard the holy man of God
Pronounce the benediction on their love :
"Whom God hath joined together let no man
Dare put asunder," and the solemn words
Re-echoed from the dark'ning walls and aisles,
Acquiring thence a new solemnity.
Within the shadow of the lectern knelt
Gerald. His locks were faintly tinged with gray
And o'er his face the furrow-marks of Time
Had crept, though stealthily. There, by his side,
A matron, fair as the Madonna, knelt,
Her eyes uplifted, and her countenance
All radiant with rays of heavenly light.
Before them kneeled the idols of their hearts ;
His rosy-featured boy to manhood grown ;
Her fair-haired daughter grown to womanhood,
And on their brows the light of happy love,
Of pure devotion shone. Yet not more pure
Than that which sanctified the hearts of those,
Their parents, who upon the Christmas Eve
Long years before had parted, and in tears.
"Ah, Gerald," whispered she with tenderness,
"This moment brings requital for the past,
That oneness God long since denied to us
He gives to ours, and thus once more unites
Our hearts." Then Gerald fixed his gaze
Upon that face—it still was dear to him,
And murmured "Peace at last ! a perfect peace.
Our God in Heaven doeth all things well."

INDEX.

The Halcyon's Return	5
Sub Ulmis	56
My Castles	57
The Voudoux and their Charms	58
"Merry Christmas"	61
The Carpet-Bagger's Soliloquy	62
An Audience in the Dark	63
"Oh! Perfectly Sober"	65
To a Child Waking from Sleep	66
An Acrostic	67
Sophronissima; or, the Vagrom's Comprehension	68
Over the Seas	76
A Louisiana Bayou Scene	77
Thomas Cat in Trouble	84
The Story of the Church Tower	86
The Tragic Mews	112
Shakspeare Modernized	113
The Imp in the Clock	115
Biloxi	118
The Maple Leaf	128
The Bliss of Boarding	129
A Local Sketch in Verse	134
On the River	138
The Requital	142

www.ingramcontent.com/pod-product-compliance
Lightning Source LLC
Chambersburg PA
CBHW030435190426
43202CB00036B/1287